GLORIOUS Mess

FROM BROKEN
TO BOLD & BEAUTIFUL

MARY MCCULLOUGH

GLORIOUS Mess

FROM BROKEN
TO BOLD & BEAUTIFUL

REDEMPTION PRESS

Published by Redemption Press, PO Box 427, Enumclaw, WA 98022.

Toll-Free (844) 2REDEEM (273-3336)

Redemption Press is honored to present this title in partnership with the author. The views expressed or implied in this work are those of the author. Redemption Press provides our imprint seal representing design excellence, creative content, and high quality production.

All Scripture quotations, unless otherwise indicated, are taken from the *Holy Bible, New International Version*®. *NIV*®. Copyright © 1973, 1978, 1984 by International Bible Society. Used by permission of Zondervan. All rights reserved.

Scripture quotations marked MSG are taken from *The Message*. Copyright © 1993, 1994, 1995, 1996, 2000, 2001, 2002. Used by permission of NavPress Publishing Group.

Scripture quotations marked NLT are taken from the Holy Bible, New Living Translation, copyright © 1996, 2004, 2015 by Tyndale House Foundation. Used by permission of Tyndale House Publishers Inc., Carol Stream, Illinois 60188. All rights reserved.

ISBN 13: 978-1-68314-206-5 (Paperback)
978-1-68314-366-6 (ePub)
978-1-68314-787-9 (Mobi)

Library of Congress Catalog Card Number: 2019912466

I dedicate this book to my GFFs (God First Friends). You are a gift from God, and I couldn't have made it through my messes without your love and support as you shared your own stories of God's faithfulness. Thank you for helping me find His glory in my story.

And to anyone who has felt the pain of a broken spirit, may the words God penned through my journey richly bless and bring healing to your spirit as well.

CONTENTS

PREFACE

Thank you for reading this GFF book. GFF is a ministry designed to encourage, equip, and empower women to put God first in all areas of their lives. It is a ministry of accountability, mentoring, and relationship. As such, you are encouraged to do this study with at least one other person or within a small group. Throughout the study I may refer to your accountability group or partner as a GFF, knowing this is perhaps not what you call your group but as a means of expressing the notion of growing in community.

Accountability has power, as evidenced in Matthew 5:14–16 (MSG):

Here's another way to put it: You're here to be light, bringing out the God-colors in the world. God is not a secret to be kept. We're going public with this, as public as a city on a hill. If I make you light-bearers, you don't think I'm going to hide you under a bucket, do you? I'm putting you on a light stand. Now that I've put you there on a hilltop, on a light stand—shine! Keep open house; be generous with your lives. *By opening up to others, you'll prompt people to open up with God, this generous Father in heaven.* (Emphasis added.)

By coming together and sharing your story with other women, you will encourage and empower them to embrace their life circumstances and find God's heart of love.

If you meet with a partner or small group, I encourage you to do so with integrity and confidentiality. Your story is *your* story. You may share it for God's glory. However, sharing someone else's story is gossip and has no place in the life of a GFF. Also, it is not necessary to divulge all the details of your story, because some places on our journeys are just too personal. But be as honest with one another as you can while respecting one another's hearts, even the heart of one who has hurt you.

In the back of the book, you will find a GFF covenant for this study. A covenant is a promise. I invite you to enter it willingly, ready to serve one another and grow together. Whether you are meeting together solely for the duration of this study or your time together spans into the future, you and your GFFs may decide to sign this covenant as a promise to care for one another lovingly and honestly.

As you sign your covenant, read it carefully, considering what you are promising. Pray together for God's strength and grace to hold each other accountable.

May God bless the binding of your hearts with His.

Mary

INTRODUCTION

If you have experienced rejection or ridicule, found your heart wounded and longing for wholeness, or ached from brokenness, you will find comfort and guidance as you journey through this study. *Glorious Mess* is an interactive study designed to help you address the broken and barren places in your heart. Life gets messy, but God longs to work in your situations to reveal His character and display His glory.

This study is set up to help you commune with God each day of the week. Over the next six weeks, we will look at common themes found in Hannah's story, such as compassion, perseverance, authentic relationship, faithfulness, and redemption. These themes will all point us to the character of God. You will meet the God of faithfulness, forgiveness, healing, love, and redemption. As we go forward I will also share lessons from my journey. I pray that these stories will help you open up to God and others.

If you use this book as a group study, during your first meeting I encourage you to become familiar with the format of the study by reading and completing the introduction together. You may also wish to sign the covenant found in the back of the book as a means of accountability to your small group or partner.

On subsequent days you may work on the lessons independently while making time to meet at a convenient time with your GFFs or study partner(s) to discuss your wonderings and insights.

Each day you will spend time looking at Hannah's story and various Scriptures that reveal God's character. The material for each of the first six days has four segments:

- A lesson enables you to delve into the Scriptures.
- Make It Personal encourages you to spend time reflecting on your own life and how the Scriptures apply to you.
- And So, We Pray helps you talk with God.
- A Discussion Question for the day's lesson invites you to either ponder and journal for yourself or prepare to discuss when you get together with your study group.

On the seventh day you will take time for Rest and Reflection to determine how you will begin applying the week's lessons to your life.

Don't worry if you miss a day. Some days' portions are shorter and can be combined. Allow yourself grace if you fall behind. Your focus is not on completion; it is on intimacy with God. You may even choose to spend more than one day on a particular lesson. The key is to handle the lessons in a way that helps you grow.

Sharing your stories, questions, and needs generates power. In a group study with your GFFs, you will carry out your covenant to one another as you come together to discuss each lesson and share your difficulties and progress. Trust God to use your honesty and generosity with one another to build intimacy among you.

Throughout the study you will find prayers. At times the prayers will be written for you. Other times I have allotted open space for you to write your personal prayers. Be honest, open, and expectant that God hears, cares, and will answer your prayers. You will see God's faithfulness in your life as you journey with Hannah.

I love Hannah's story, and she is one of my favorite biblical women. During my years of knowing and walking with God, I have been encouraged and energized by various aspects of her story. She was authentic. She was broken. She was barren in spirit. And she journeyed with God even when her heart wasn't in it. Hannah was ridiculed and mocked. She grew weary, but she never gave up. She was a beautiful woman of grace.

Hannah shows us how to go on when the circumstances around us scream, "Just give up already!" Hannah points us toward the God who is faithful, patient, and intimate. Her story will encourage and equip you to take this faith walk with strength and joy.

At your first meeting focus on becoming familiar with the Scriptures used in this study. Just take in the words, the tone, and the setting. You may even choose to read the Bible portion aloud so you are engaged as you hear God's Word spoken to you. As you read, listen for His still, small voice bringing light to various aspects of the Scripture. Encouragement, questions, or personal insight may come to your mind. Don't dismiss these stirrings, because through them God's Spirit may be making you aware of some aspect of your life. On the other hand, you may not feel a nudge at all, which is perfectly fine. Faith is knowing God is near even when you don't feel Him.

Hannah's name means grace and favor. Now it is time to unfold her story and discover why her name suits her so well. Let's begin by reading 1 Samuel 1:1–2:11 as this will be our focus over the next six weeks. As you read, write your initial thoughts or questions. Don't worry about right or wrong responses. Just write what comes to your mind when you hear and read the Scriptures. Note what you feel and wonder.

I still believe

_____

_____

_____

_____

_____

_____

_____

_____

Once you've taken time to read and record your thoughts, discuss your ideas and questions with your GFFs. Jot their thoughts and comments in the space provided below.

_____

_____

_____

_____

_____

_____

_____

_____

Continue to refer to your initial thoughts and questions throughout the next six weeks. As you move through the study, portions of history and aspects of Hannah's story will become clearer and more applicable to your life.

Week 1

Change is hard at first, messy in the middle, and gorgeous at the end.
—Robin Sharma

This week you will begin unfolding Hannah's story and opening
your heart to embrace your own glorious messes.

Day 1
A Glorious Mess

And we know that in all things God works for the good of those
who love him, who have been called according to his purpose.
—Romans 8:28

I'm guessing that as you decided to begin this study, you were
intrigued by the oxymoronic title *Glorious Mess,* two radically opposite
concepts brought together to represent one idea. As you move through
this study, you will begin to more fully understand and hopefully embrace
the idea of a glorious mess.

You will meet Hannah, a woman who felt unloved and incomplete
without a child. She let the world determine her value. Her enemy,
relentless in her taunting, left Hannah unable to stand under the pain.
Hannah was the wife of a shared husband. She wept. She cried. She lost
her appetite. Basically, Hannah was a mess. And if we are being honest
with ourselves, aren't we all a little messy? Rather, aren't we all a *lot* messy?

Fortunately, we don't have to get all cleaned up before we go to God.
He loves us while we are in our messes and as we move through them.
He sees us from His glorious perspective, and if we allow it He will use

our difficulties to display His glory. Therefore I've started calling each problem I bring to God a "glorious mess."

Every situation you face has been allowed by God. He has seen each one and knows it can make you more mature in your faith if you allow Him to finish His work in you as He brings you through.

Friend, I want you to know that God never wastes an opportunity to teach you and to grow your faith. He will use every poor choice, every act of unkindness, and every painful situation for your good. He is not only the God of the wonderfully amazing things in our lives. He is also the God of the messes.

Messes can originate from your own decisions, fears, and insecurities, from the hand of someone else intent on harming you, or through the indirect consequences of another's foolishness. Regardless of the origin, you may find yourself in a pit of despair.

Nevertheless, all your situations are in God's hands. He never loses sight of you. He never shakes His head, ashamed of you. He never leaves the seat of His throne to pace and stew over how He can work out a situation. He watches and waits until the perfect time of deliverance. He walks with you, holds you, and cheers you on as you find your way to victory. Friend, please know that your trials are not in vain. And through Hannah, you can learn how to let the messiness be redeemed for God's glory.

This week you are beginning a journey of self-reflection and change. Be real, be honest, be changed.

You will see that Hannah handed her mess to God, and He made it into something glorious, not for Hannah's glory but for His. Romans 8:28 says, "And we know that in all things God works for the good of those who love him, who have been called according to his purpose." How does it make you feel to know that God is working for your good?

_____

_____

_____

_____

Make It Personal

What "glorious messes" do you need to hand over to God so He can transform them and receive the glory? Are you ready to get real with God? Maybe you have messes you tried to leave in the past, but they continue to linger today. Maybe your children have made poor choices, your marriage is rocky at best, or your finances are spiraling out of control. Or perhaps you have an addiction or tend to gossip. No matter what the mess or how big you think it is, God can redeem it if you hand it over to Him.

_____

_____

_____

_____

And So, We Pray

Dear Lord, like Hannah, I am a glorious mess. Today I am making the first step to hand over:

_____

_____

_____

I'm sorry for the choices I've made to create this mess. Help me also to forgive others who play a part in my mess. I trust You to use my mess for Your glory. Amen.

Day 1 Discussion Question

God is not just God of the good. He is God over every situation. A common misconception about being a Christian is that you have to have your life in order before you can go to God. Yet Hannah's story will show you that God longs to be in relationship with you and is present with you through the good, the bad, and the ugly. Is this a new perspective for you? Talk about your perspective of God in relation to the circumstances of your life.

Day 2
LOVED UNIQUELY

There was a certain man from Ramathaim, a Zuphite from the hill country of Ephraim, whose name was Elkanah son of Jeroham, the son of Elihu, the son of Tohu, the son of Zuph, an Ephraimite.
—1 Samuel 1:1

This week we meet the key characters in Hannah's story and gain insight into the culture of the time. In today's verse we meet Elkanah, Hannah's husband.

If you're like me, you may have been tempted to skip over the genealogy mentioned in the above verse, but it is included to establish that Elkanah came from a long line of families devoted to God. It's important to note that the listing of his family lineage not only establishes the Bible as having historical accuracy but also gives credibility to the fact that biblical characters were real, not fictional. This lineage also reveals God's faithful commitment to generations of His people.

Yet more profound is the phrase, "There was a certain man," calling us to an awareness that God not only sees the long line of family groups, but He also has His eye on each individual person. Throughout the Bible

God identifies people by name and tells their particular story. He notices the details. He hears the specific cry of each child's heart and responds to each one individually because there are no cookie cutter molds when it comes to God's children. Each one is special. Each one is unique.

God knows you by name too. Matthew 10:30 says, "And even the very hairs on your head are all numbered." You are unique and special to God. He sees and notices you among the millions of people on this earth. You are loved uniquely.

Make It Personal

As I pen these words, I remember the first time I attended an NFL game. Throngs of fans wedged through the gate toward the stadium seats. I felt small and unimportant among the sea of blue jerseys in a stadium prepared for some 67,000 fans. Yet in the same moment, I was in awe of the fact that God knew me personally.

Like Elkanah and me, you are not just one person in a crowd. You are uniquely loved by God. What thoughts and feelings stir within you, knowing the God of the universe loves you? What special traits and set of skills do you possess that make you unique?

_____

_____

_____

_____

And So, We Pray

Dear God, when I try to imagine the fullness of Your love for me, I am overwhelmed; however, I'm forever grateful that You chose to create me individually among many. You're intentional in knowing and pursuing me. Not only do You know me by name, but You want me just as I am. Help me to intentionally choose You daily and to desire the same relationship with You that You desire with me. Amen.

Day 2 Discussion Question

Today you were introduced to Elkanah as "a certain man," and were presented with the idea that God saw and loved him as an individual. Talk about what implications this has for you.

Day 3
Embracing Your Messes

He had two wives; one was called Hannah and the other Peninnah.
Peninnah had children, but Hannah had none.
—1 Samuel 1:2

And there it is . . . the makings of a glorious mess. Right here, already, in verse number two of Hannah's story, we see trouble brewing. I guess you made note of the fact that Hannah was one of Elkanah's *two* wives.

We know that polygamy was a customary practice at that time in history. Barren women frequently gave a servant girl to their husbands for the purpose of bearing children and ensuring future generations. Additionally, unmarried or widowed women were taken as subsequent wives to married men, who would then provide for their basic needs. Married or not, women whom men did not take in were left destitute and vulnerable. Although having multiple wives was not God's design, it was a customary practice. But this practice did not come without cost and disruption to the family unit.

Notice that God did not choose to use a picture-perfect family to tell His story. He chose flawed, normal, everyday people just like you and me. Elkanah had two wives, which created its own set of challenges. Today as well, many relationships are chaotic and dysfunctional. Healthy relationships require effort and loads of grace, yet even the best relationships get messy at times.

Thankfully, God sees beyond messes to the hearts of His children and works within these messes to reveal Himself today just as He did thousands of years ago in the Bible stories. Human weaknesses and failures are not the focus of the stories; rather they are used to magnify the grace and glory of God.

Make It Personal

I am a recovering perfectionist. What I mean is I spent a lot of my life feeling that I had to earn God's favor by following the rules. When I failed, I vowed to work harder at being flawless and hid my hurts and fears because I felt they were signs of weakness. I worked hard to keep everything and everyone in my life in order.

But when health issues, poor choices, financial strains, and broken relationships left me barren and broken, I began seeing that God was still faithful even though my life was in disarray. Ironically, it was when I lost control and embraced the messiness of my life that I found freedom. God's glory was greater than my messes!

How about you? Can you relate to the life that you read about in today's lesson? Do you find comfort in knowing that your messes do not disqualify you from God's love but rather will become a tool through which He will show you the fullness of His glory? He will transform your story into an amazing glory.

_____

_____

_____

_____

And So, We Pray

Dear God, thank You for accepting me as I am. Help me to be honest with myself and with my accountability partner about my mistakes and messes so I can see Your glory. Use Hannah and Elkanah's story to help me find healing for my relationships and hope for my future. Amen.

Day 3 Discussion Question

When introduced to Hannah, you became fully aware of the messiness of her life and the fact that her difficulties didn't disqualify her from God's love but rather made her a perfect instrument through which He could reveal His greatness.

Have you ever felt your messiness was too great for God to forgive or to heal? If you feel comfortable with your group, share the areas where you need God's healing.

Day 4
YEAR AFTER YEAR

Year after year this man went up from his town to worship and
sacrifice to the LORD Almighty at Shiloh.
—1 Samuel 1:3

The phrase "year after year" signifies that Elkanah was
a faithful follower of the Lord throughout his life. As you remember
from a previous lesson, Elkanah came from a long family line of believers
and most likely studied the Scriptures, rituals, and practices of the faith
from childhood. As an adult, Elkanah practiced his faith and taught his
family to do so as well.

By law and as part of the traditions Elkanah practiced, the Israelite
males were required to attend three annual festivals. Although women
and children were not required to attend, many families traveled together
to worship and offer sacrifices to the Lord.

Like Elkanah, you may have grown up in a family where you
experienced rich faith traditions and heard Scripture year after year. Or
maybe this is your first experience in learning about God. Either way,
year after year, God has pursued you, even when you were unaware of

His presence, and He longs to have a relationship with you through His Son, Jesus Christ. As you journey on, God will draw you deeper into His love . . . year after year.

Make It Personal

I was raised in a Christian home where attending church and studying Scripture were always a part of my life. Even though I came from a family of faith, the day came when I had to make a decision for myself about my relationship with God. What I've learned in this year-after-year journey is that regardless of my choices, God has been faithful to me.

What is your story? Are you just beginning a faith journey, are you returning to God after a time of wandering, or are you one who has journeyed with God year after year? Take some time to journal about your story.

_____

_____

_____

_____

_____

_____

_____

And So, We Pray

Use the space provided to write your own prayer, thanking God for pursuing you year after year.

_____

_____

_____

_____

_____

_____

_____

_____

_____

Day 4 Discussion Question

Elkanah had journeyed with God for many years. Talk about your personal faith journey. Whether you are new to the faith or you have experienced God's presence for many years, this is a great time to begin talking with your group about your experience with God. What can you share with your group about your personal faith journey?

Day 5
GOD FIRST

Year after year this man went up from his town to worship and
sacrifice to the LORD Almighty at Shiloh, where Hophni and
Phinehas, the two sons of Eli, were priests of the LORD.
—1 Samuel 1:3

Just as we are discovering Elkanah's faithfulness to God, the
Scripture takes a twist and introduces us to Hophni and Phinehas, sons
of Eli, the high priest. Hophni and Phinehas were corrupt, wicked men
known for stealing from those who offered sacrifices at the temple. As the
people brought sacrifices, Hophni and Phinehas would reserve the best
portions for themselves, cheating God and the ones sacrificing to Him.

The placement of the phrase "where Hophni and Phinehas, the
two sons of Eli, were priests of the LORD" insinuates that Hophni and
Phinehas's reputation as evil men was known throughout the nation. Yet
their disloyalty to God did not stop Elkanah from making the annual
trip to offer sacrifices to the Lord.

Attending the annual festivals was a difficult task and required not
only a physical sacrifice to burn on the altar but also a sacrifice of time

and much physical exertion to travel to the tabernacle. Yet Elkanah made a decision to live his life in a way that pleased God regardless of what others thought or did. Hophni and Phinehas's vile presence at the tabernacle could have been reason enough to stay home each year, but Elkanah chose to put God first. His desire to be obedient outweighed all the obstacles in his path.

Make It Personal

I have to admit that there have been times when I allowed others to hinder my actions in service and submission to God. At times I have chosen to make excuses for not doing the godly thing because it was inconvenient or difficult. I pray for a faith like Elkanah's—I pray for a faith that forges on when faced with opposition, keeping God first.

How about you? What obstacles are you facing that keep you from pursuing God? What barriers stand in the way of making a breakthrough in your faith to truly serve God first? Check all that apply:

- ☐ Relationship(s)
- ☐ Time
- ☐ Lack of support for your faith journey
- ☐ A situation/circumstance (either past or present)
- ☐ Fear
- ☐ Other

You may choose to use the space below to journal about the barriers you face.

_____

_____

_____

_____

_____

And So, We Pray

Dear God, please forgive me for the times I have chosen to allow others to influence my faithfulness to You. Forgive me for not standing firm in the face of opposition and trials. I ask that You strengthen me and give me the desire and ability to keep You first in my life. Amen.

Day 5 Discussion Question

Elkanah chose to put God first even in the face of opposition. What trials and challenges have you experienced or are currently experiencing that make pursuing a relationship with God seem difficult?

Day 6

WAYWARD, YET LOVED

> And if he finds it, truly I tell you, he is happier about that one
> sheep than about the ninety-nine that did not wander off. In the
> same way your Father in heaven is not willing that any of these
> little ones should perish.
> —Matthew 18:13–14

Let's take a moment to meet Eli, the high priest, and take a look at his sons, Hophni and Phinehas. As chief priest Eli was responsible for overseeing the daily workings of the tabernacle.

Eli was well along in his years at the time this passage in 1 Samuel was written. Thus, as tradition would have it, his sons were assigned to help their father. One of their responsibilities was to accept the sacrifices that the faithful brought into the temple. Though these men were literally raised in the tabernacle with traditions and scriptural knowledge being part of their everyday life, 1 Samuel 2:12 says, "Eli's sons were scoundrels; they had no regard for the LORD." Unfortunately, they knew the ways of God, but they did not love and honor Him.

Eli's sons appeared to have everything necessary to become men of God: knowledge of the Scriptures, access to teachings and traditions, and a father who served the Lord. However, they lacked the one thing God desires: a relationship. God longs for all His children to choose to live in a loving relationship with Him. Though God chose to love these two men, they chose not to respond to His love.

In Matthew 18, we find a parable of God's love for His wayward children. This passage illustrates Jesus as the shepherd looking for His lost sheep. And, oh, how He rejoices when God finds one of His lost sheep! The lost sheep matter.

Make It Personal

Hophni and Phineas were wayward, yet God still loved them. Thankfully, God didn't give up on me when I chose poorly. He didn't quit loving me when I lived outside His will. Though I did reap the consequences of my choices, God sought me out and continues to do so each time my wandering heart leads me astray. And He does the same for you. What He desires is a repentant heart, a heart that seeks forgiveness, and a desire to be changed.

Take time to ponder your current situation in life. Are you living a lifestyle outside of God, much like Hophni and Phineas? Are there changes you feel you should make in order to grow in your relationship with God? God loves you just as you are, right where you are, but your choices can become hindrances to your relationship with God. Consider journaling your thoughts here.

_____

_____

_____

_____

_____

_____

Regardless of where you find yourself today, you are completely loved by God. As a shepherd who searches for His wayward sheep, God has His eye of love on you.

And So, We Pray

You may use this space to write your own prayer today. Perhaps there are areas where you need to ask God's forgiveness.

_____

_____

_____

_____

Day 6 Discussion Question

Hophni and Phineas made choices that did not align with God's will for their lives, yet God loved them and wanted a relationship with them. The parable of the lost sheep reminds us that God seeks us even when we are wayward so we can repent and be in right relationship with Him.

What areas of your life need repentance or healing?

Day 7
REST AND REFLECTION

Today is a day to spend time with the Lord in any way you desire. You may choose to meditate on a Scripture from the previous week, summarize your thoughts, list your questions, or just sit quietly with the Lord. You may wish to read your Bible.

Use the space below to journal, sketch, or otherwise record your thoughts. Handwrite a Scripture or phrase. Or just take this time to sit quietly with God.

Week 2

Ewww . . . you got bitterness and jealousy all over my happiness!
—Cindy Brady

This week will focus on character and being a woman of grace
and beauty even in the middle of trials.

COSTLY COMPETITION

Because the Lord had closed Hannah's womb, her rival kept
provoking her in order to irritate her. This went on year after year.
Whenever Hannah went up to the house of the Lord, her rival
provoked her till she wept and would not eat.
—1 Samuel 1:6–7

Read 1 Samuel 1:6–7 slowly, focusing on each word. Look
for an identifiable tone or topic within the passage. You may write your
thoughts here.

_____

_____

_____

_____

Perhaps you sense the tension in these verses. Do you see the taunting
and jealousy going on between Peninnah and Hannah? It seems as if

Peninnah was very cruel, hateful, and uncaring. Hannah did not deserve such treatment. Why would someone ever make fun of a woman who could not bear a child?

Peninnah possessed something Hannah didn't, and she made sure Hannah knew it. Peninnah bore children for Elkanah, and her social value was measured by the birth of her sons. Culturally, Peninnah was respected, but Hannah was not. Hannah's barrenness had major cultural implications. As a matter of fact, in her culture, being unable to bear children was a sign of failure and even grounds for divorce.

During this time in Old Testament history, Hannah was an outcast. Bearing children was a woman's purpose, and because she could not, Hannah was barren in more than just her womb. Her very soul ached.

Sadly, Hannah's torment wasn't a short-term issue. Year after year, Peninnah provoked Hannah. Reread 1 Samuel 1:6. Why did Peninnah provoke Hannah?

_____

_____

_____

Seriously? Did we read that correctly? Peninnah provoked Hannah to "irritate her." Can you imagine such spite? Peninnah went out of her way to cause pain. She intentionally reminded Hannah that God had closed her womb, leaving her unable to bear the precious children she longed for. My heart bleeds for Hannah. Oh, the immense pain she must have suffered!

Read 1 Samuel 1:7. What was Hannah's response to the ridicule?

_____

_____

Exactly as we might expect, Hannah wept uncontrollably and was unable to eat. Her deep emotional wounds were constantly torn open and pain-filled grooves were worn deep in her heart and mind because of the constant ridicule. It was too much to bear. Hannah lived in tears, pain, and a pit of sorrow she never expected.

Unfortunately, much like Peninnah, women today can be cruel, unkind, and harsh with one another. We judge other moms because their children aren't well behaved. We comment that their children are too close in age for our liking or that they are not mothering to our standards. Not uncommonly, a woman points out another woman's weaknesses in an attempt to diminish her beautiful strengths. As evidenced in Hannah's story, competition among women is a dangerous and divisive tool of the Enemy.

Paul, a follower of Christ and the greatest of apostles, teaches us how to talk to and about each other. Read Ephesians 4:29 to find a better way to respond to the women in your life. "Do not let any unwholesome talk come out of your mouths, but only what is helpful for building others up according to their needs, that it may benefit those who listen."

I assume that at some point in our lives, we have all walked in both Peninnah and Hannah's shoes. We have both given and received ridicule. However, as we observe the consequences of ridicule through Hannah's story, may we heed Paul's instructions. Let us learn life lessons from these Scriptures for the betterment of our relationships and lives.

Make It Personal

Have you ever felt uncomfortable around other women? Did you feel intimidated by their beauty, family, lifestyle, or various assets? Sometimes when we feel threatened (truly or perceived) by other women, we look for the weakest, most vulnerable aspects of their lives to attack. We ridicule, gossip about, and highlight their flaws. Rather than reach out in compassion and encouragement, we set out to diminish others to protect our public images and hide our own faults. God does not desire any of His daughters to develop such hardness of heart.

Have you been provoked or intimidated like Hannah was by other women (either intentionally or perceived)? How did you respond?

_____

_____

_____

_____

Have you, like Peninnah, ridiculed another woman either openly or in your mind? It can be hard to admit or even see the worst in ourselves, but look within and be honest with yourself. The only way to change your heart is to let God change your mind about your behavior. Being changed is the desired outcome of intimacy with God.

_____

_____

_____

_____

Tomorrow we will look a little closer at this rivalry and see further what Jesus has to say about it.

And So, We Pray

Dear Jesus, forgive us for the times we haven't been compassionate with other women. Help us to find our worth in You so we can confidently praise and encourage others rather than shrink back in fear and intimidation. Lord, break our hearts for others' needs and enable us to be women of encouragement. Amen.

Day 1 Discussion Question

How have comparison and compassion played out in your life? (Be careful not to specify names when sharing your story.) Why is comparison so dangerous in the life of a Christian?

Day 2
DANGEROUS PRIDE

Make a careful exploration of who you are and the work you have
been given, and then sink yourself into that. Don't be impressed
with yourself. Don't compare yourself with others. Each of you
must take responsibility for doing the creative best you can with
your own life.
—Galatians 6:4–5 MSG

Peninnah provoked Hannah because of her
barrenness. Perhaps, as Peninnah played with her children, she gave
Hannah a subtle, arrogant smile as Hannah sat alone watching and
longing to hold a child of her own. Imagine Peninnah's small talk and
petty, disdainful comments about Hannah's inadequacies.

On the other hand, it might have been not her words but her actions
that caused Hannah's pain. Regardless of how Peninnah provoked
Hannah, it was not godly.

Have you ever had that experience? Someone knows your weaknesses
or insecurities and reminds you of them every time you are in her

presence? Or perhaps you are the one provoking others. Why do women do such terrible things? Pride.

Pride is the lack of humility. The proud are easily offended, quick to ridicule or degrade, and not dependent upon the Holy Spirit's leading. The proud feel they can live without God and take life matters into their own hands. I stated earlier that Peninnah's pride wasn't godly, but Proverbs 6:16–19 puts it this way:

> There are six things the LORD hates, seven that are detestable to him; haughty eyes, a lying tongue, hands that shed innocent blood, a heart that devises wicked schemes, feet that are quick to rush into evil, a false witness who pours out lies and a person who stirs up conflict in the community.

God hates pride. Therefore if we are striving to place God first in all we do, we must deal with pride. This leaves us seeking an answer to the question, How do we avoid the pride God detests?

Galatians 6:4–5 (MSG) says:

> Make a careful exploration of who you are and the work you have been given, and then sink yourself into that. Don't be impressed with yourself. Don't compare yourself with others. Each of you must take responsibility for doing the creative best you can with your own life.

Peninnah focused much more on belittling Hannah than on dealing with her own pride. And isn't this often the case? We can see the pride in others, but we don't see it in ourselves. This is a tendency in us that Jesus had to address (Matthew 7:5). But, my friend, this book is about you and me, not about others. You can't change the prideful gal at your children's school, the arrogant lady in your small group, or the condescending colleague. But you can pray for changes in yourself.

Begin by humbling yourself and asking God to convict you of areas in your life where you hold pride.

The conviction you need will come from the soft nudges of your heart and speak gently in the form of "I was wrong" or "I shouldn't have said that." It may be the soft reminder of a Scripture verse or passage. Conviction leads you to repentance—that means saying you are wrong and God's way is right. Repentance draws you closer to God.

Condemnation, on the other hand, brings shame and diminishes your spirit. It pushes you away from God. It sounds more like these: "You failed again." "You're so rude." "You'll never get this right." Condemnation is not from God. Knowing the difference allows us to refuse to accept condemnation, choosing instead to repent and draw closer to God as He changes us.

Make It Personal

Many times God has convicted me of pride. Oh, not the in-your-face, bold, speak-your-mind kind of pride, but rather a subtle pride that stirs up unkind thoughts and a bitter taste of resentment. A pride that damages relationships from the inside out.

If we seek in prayer to be convicted of pride, then God will open our eyes. Begin making notes of when your feelings are hurt. What makes you bristle or shoot back with a defensive comment or jeer? When do you find yourself explaining your behavior instead of offering an apology? Are there situations from which you will not retreat and people from whom you just won't back down? Do you put up walls of arrogance that keep others at bay? Or is your heart tender enough to let others see the real you?

_____

_____

_____

And So, We Pray

Dear Lord, today I ask You to speak to my heart. Open my mind to see the places in my life where there are arrogance and pride. Whether it's in my looks, career, parenting, or children, Lord, reveal it to me so I may be humble in spirit. Give me the courage to face my pride head on and deal with it. Amen.

Take a few moments to let God speak to you in answer to your prayer. Make note of what God shows you. What areas of your life, if any, do you feel God prompting you to work on accepting or changing? Remember that prayer isn't always answered immediately. God may open your heart to a situation when you are in it or at another time. He may recall a Scripture to your mind, nudging you to make a change. You have invited His Spirit into your life, and you are a work in progress.

Day 2 Discussion Question

Peninnah's pride was rooted in the fact that she could bear children and Hannah could not. Yet it was God who allowed Peninnah to bear children. It was nothing of her doing. What do you believe is the difference between pride and godly confidence?

Day 3
COMPASSIONATE WORDS

*Gracious words are a honeycomb, sweet to the soul
and healing to the bones.*
—Proverbs 16:24

We read yesterday of Peninnah being an irritation to Hannah. Peninnah's character is definitely in question. She could have had an entirely different story written about her. We could have read about how Peninnah saw the brokenness in Hannah's heart and helped her find healing. Or we could have marveled at how she talked with Hannah compassionately and sat with her when she cried. Wouldn't it have been an incredible story to read of Peninnah and Hannah working together to raise Elkanah's children? Instead we read of Peninnah's competition with Hannah and her hard-heartedness.

We often take our spoken words lightly. However, Scripture warns us that we will all give an account for the words we speak (Mark 12:36). We are also told that our words have the power to kill or bring life (Proverbs

18:21). Friend, did you hear that? Our words can kill others. Oh, not physically, but we can certainly kill another's spirit.

I know you've witnessed murder by mouth. Perhaps you've witnessed it at the supermarket as a mother demeaned her child's behavior in public. You've seen the teenage boy berated by his parent because he made an error playing basketball. Or a spouse's joking turned to embarrassment and pain. Maybe you've been the recipient or, unfortunately, the abuser. Words are powerful.

Proverbs 16:24 says, "Gracious words are a honeycomb, sweet to the soul and healing to the bones." What power lies within words tempered with grace?

_____

_____

_____

Peninnah could have used her words to bring healing to Hannah's heart and soul. You and I have the same choice. When we encounter other women, we can choose words of grace by complimenting, encouraging, and speaking value into their day. To do this we have to continue asking God to remove our pride. Work at humbling yourself so you can see the best in others. Make encouragement a habit.

Contrary to the world's ways, you don't have to tear people down to feel good about yourself. Complimenting others frees you to be satisfied with both them and yourself. You will fill any void in your heart as you pour out true love onto others.

Make It Personal

Respond to this statement with a simple yes or no: "I am an encourager and cheerleader for other women, even those I don't know."

_____

Hannah lost sight of who she was in the Lord and allowed Peninnah to become the god that dictated her worth. Peninnah also had a false sense of her own worth because culture deemed her worthy for bearing children. Her self-worth was defined by those around her, not God. Friend, know that your worth does not lessen when people around you fail to recognize your value.

I have walked in Hannah's shoes, allowing others to define my self-worth. This rough road dead-ended in severe depression and anxiety, at which point I was unable to cheer for anyone else because my self-image was so poor. This was not the road God intended for me to take.

Take a moment to be honest with yourself. Ask God to help you truly evaluate the way you love yourself because it will be the foundation for how you love others.

If either of these women had known their value to God, we would have been reading an entirely different story. Can you accept yourself for who you are at this moment, flaws and all? Do you know your value in Christ, or do your determine your worth by your achievements, status, or the perceptions of those around you?

Why should we focus on this question? Because if we are insecure in our identity in Christ, we will struggle to help others find theirs. The more we realize our need for a Savior, the more our compassionate acts and gracious words will spill out onto others.

And So, We Pray

Lord, please give me the courage to step out and encourage another woman today. Help me to respond in true humility as I look beyond the exterior into the precious hearts of Your daughters. Amen.

Day 3 Discussion Questions

Words are powerful. What are some ways a woman of God can use her words to empower and encourage other women? What are some areas where a woman of God must be alert to the dangers of her speech?

Day 4
A BITTER ROOT OF JEALOUSY

You're blessed when you're content with just who you are—no more, no less. That's the moment you find yourselves proud owners of everything that can't be bought.
—Matthew 5:5 MSG

We've spent the last few days looking at Peninnah's seemingly callous heart. We've seen how Peninnah provoked Hannah to tears because of her barren womb. We hurt for Hannah. But what if Peninnah's heart was also hurting? What if her provocations resulted from her bitter jealousy, her own wounds and scars? Let's look a little closer.

First Samuel 1:5 says, "But to Hannah he gave a double portion because he loved her, and the LORD had closed her womb." Why did Elkanah give Hannah a double portion of meat as his sacrifice?

_____

_____

Elkanah deeply loved Hannah. Scripture doesn't tell us that he didn't love Peninnah, but I think it's safe to assume that his love for Hannah was greater than his love for Peninnah. Maybe Peninnah was broken too. Perhaps she was jealous of the love Elkanah had for Hannah.

How dangerous and damaging jealousy can be.

Proverbs 27:4 says, "Anger is cruel and fury overwhelming, but who can stand before jealousy?" Try summarizing this passage in your own words.

_____

_____

_____

_____

Anger is often thought to be the strongest, most damaging emotion. Just think how angry a woman can become and how harmful her actions in her rage. Yet this verse asks us, Who can bear jealousy? To bear means to stand up under the weight of something. Jealousy is a heavy burden we heap upon ourselves. You can't see it, but it's there. Jealousy eats us from the inside out. It displaces our joy and contentment with a never satisfied yearning for that which we don't already possess.

To get another glimpse of jealousy in action from the Bible, let's look at another pair of women. Their names are Sarah and Hagar. You can read their entire account in Genesis 16–21. In the meantime, I'll give you a quick summary.

Sarah, Abraham's wife, could not bear children, so in her impatience she gave her servant girl, Hagar, to Abraham so he could have children through her. Now this seemed like a great plan to Sarah at the time, but after Hagar bore this sweet baby boy, she began to taunt Sarah. Hagar's taunting fueled Sarah's tiny bit of jealousy like gas on a wildfire in the dry heat of July—and a woman's fury can blaze like wildfire. Sarah blamed Abraham for the mess and treated Hagar so harshly that she ran away to die in the desert. At the prompting of the Lord, Hagar returned home only to be thrown out later due to Sarah's wildfire jealousy.

In this story jealousy dominated, damaging both women, their spouse, their children, and their nation—even to this day. So the question posed earlier is truly relevant. Who can bear jealousy?

God always gives us a better way to live. Jesus tells us that we are blessed when we are content. And being content means knowing Jesus loves you. Contentment isn't found in acceptance, possessions, accomplishments, or appearances. Scripture says, "You're blessed when you're content with just who you are—no more, no less. That's the moment you find yourselves proud owners of everything that can't be bought" (Matthew 5:5 MSG).

Make It Personal

I can't say I've experienced jealousy to the extent presented in these two stories, but I've longed for what others have. However, since I've spent more time learning who I am to God, I can say that jealousy rears its ugly head less often. I realized the change recently when I visited my friend's amazingly gorgeous new home. I left feeling happy for her instead of longing for what she had. I left feeling blessed by her blessing.

Journal your thoughts below as you sit and think about jealousy, contentment, and who you are in Christ. Keep in mind that jealousy isn't just longing for status and possessions. It is possible to long to be like someone else as well.

_____

_____

_____

_____

_____

And So, We Pray

Lord, I want this contentment. I want to be satisfied in You. Help me to find my worth and contentment in You, not the things of this earth. Help me especially with the jealousy I feel about/toward

_____. Amen.

Day 4 Discussion Question

I once read this saying: "If you love what you have, what you have is enough." To clarify, by the word *love*, the author of this quote is not implying an idolization but rather thankfulness for and valuing of what is possessed. What are some practical ways to combat jealousy?

Day 5
A Change of Mind

Do not conform to the pattern of this world, but be transformed
by the renewing of your mind. Then you will be able to test and
approve what God's will is—his good, pleasing and perfect will.
—Romans 12:2

Peninnah and Hannah were rivals, and their lives
were messed up because of it. Regardless of where the blame fell, the
competition was damaging. Peninnah's harsh actions were intended to
raise herself up and tear Hannah down.

What motivated Peninnah's actions? Her thoughts? I am no mind
reader, but I think I have a pretty good idea what Peninnah was thinking.
What will I say to Hannah at supper? How can I make her unhappy today?
She probably replayed Elkanah's kindness as he carried Hannah's water
jug, not hers. I believe her mind ran freely with thoughts that fueled
jealousy and hatred.

Sadly, it's common to see this type of destructive competition
between women even today. It's in our homes, on the job, at play, in

our social circles, and sadly even in the church. And it all begins with a single thought.

Today's verse focuses on our thoughts. Our thoughts initiate all our actions, good and bad. They control our feelings. In turn, how we feel determines how we act. So if we are going to change from being competitors to encouragers, prideful to humble, and jealous to content, we must change the way we think.

Focus on Philippians 4:8. Highlight the attributes of godly thoughts. "Finally, brothers and sisters, whatever is true, whatever is noble, whatever is right, whatever is pure, whatever is lovely, whatever is admirable—if anything is excellent or praiseworthy—think on such things."

Through Hannah's story God may have made you aware of several damaging attitudes and behaviors. When thoughts of jealousy, bitterness, or pride threaten to control your mind, rebuke them, and replace them with this verse. You have power over your thoughts. You can decide what you will think about.

When negative thoughts of yourself come to mind, replace them with the truth God says about you. As you venture on this journey of change, remember it doesn't come easily. Be patient and persistent in the battle. Use all the spiritual weapons you need to be the victor. Don't let negative or harmful thoughts about others consume your mind. Cast them aside immediately.

You can't stop thoughts from popping into your mind. But you can shut them down. You can, however, control how long they are allowed to stay. When a negative thought enters, follow it with a positive thought laced with truth. Don't let the negative have the last say. Here's what I mean: When someone speaks unkindly, you may think, *Wow, that was rude of her.* But then remind yourself that you are growing in godly speech too. Offer the grace you so readily receive for yourself.

When jealousy knocks at the door of your heart, you may think, *I wish I had a home like this.* But quickly change your thought to a praise such as, *Lord, thank You for the gift of my home.*

When another spews anger or unkindness on you, it's easy to think, *She never treats me kindly.* At that moment, retaliation may seem like the best option, but change your mind. Think, *No matter how she treats me, I will choose to treat her with love.*

When thoughts of inadequacy threaten to tear you down, replace them with what God has to say about you. His Word is truth. You can trust it and claim it. A simple thought like, *I wish I were more beautiful* should be replaced with, *God, You formed my inward parts; you knitted me together in my mother's womb. I praise you, for I am fearfully and wonderfully made* (Psalm 139:13–14, author paraphrase).

It isn't easy to change the way you think. However, it is *possible* to change your thoughts. Focus on the way God sees and treats you even when you are imperfect and messy.

Make It Personal

I am working to become more aware of what causes my sense of rivalry to flare up. Finding my triggers helps me be on alert about catching negative thoughts and turning them into positive truths.

What thoughts do you struggle with concerning other women or yourself? What specific situations or people trip you up when it comes to positive, encouraging thinking?

_____

_____

_____

_____

_____

What can you do to make a change in your thinking?

_____

_____

_____

_____

_____

_____

And So, We Pray

Lord, help me to discipline my thoughts. When envious or negative thoughts enter my mind, help me to shut them down before they cause me to act sinfully. I know I can't stop thoughts from popping into my head, but with Your help I can train my brain not to dwell on them. I ask that Your Spirit be present in my thoughts to make me an encourager of all women—me included. Amen.

Day 5 Discussion Questions

Our thoughts ultimately determine our actions. Would you say you tend to be more positive or negative in your thinking? How do you handle negative thoughts and attitudes? How can memorization of Scripture affect a believer's thinking?

Day 6
KNOWING WHOSE YOU ARE

Show me the wonders of your great love, you who save by your
right hand those who take refuge in you from their foes. Keep
me as the apple of your eye; hide me in the shadow of your wings
from the wicked who are out to destroy me, from my mortal
enemies who surround me.
—Psalm 17:7–8

Clearly Peninnah struggled with pride and jealousy.
However Hannah had a problem of her own. She didn't know her own
worth. She allowed customs and the world around her to define her
value. Have you ever felt like Hannah? Explain.

_____

_____

_____

_____

Throughout His Word God has a lot to say about your worth. Genesis 1:27 says, "So God created mankind in his own image, in the image of God he created them, male and female, he created them." Try rephrasing this passage in your own words. What does it say about your worth?

_____

_____

_____

_____

God created you in His own image. You are not merely a creation. God, the almighty Creator, loved you enough to create you in His image of perfection, holiness, and goodness.

Read Genesis 1:31 and then circle the words God used to describe His creation. "God saw all that he had made, and it was very good. And there was evening and there was morning—the sixth day."

It wasn't until God had created mankind that He said His creation was "very good." Prior to this point He described His creation as "good," but after He was delighted. Humans brought Him great joy then, and you, dear GFF, bring Him joy every moment of every day simply because you are His.

Read Psalm 17:7–8:

Show me the wonders of your great love,
    you who save by your right hand
    those who take refuge in you from their foes.
  Keep me as the apple of your eye;
    hide me in the shadow of your wings.

After reading this passage how do you believe God views you?

_____

_____

_____

_____

Yes, you are the apple of His eye. He loves you just as you are right now. You don't have to get it all together to be loved. You don't have to clean up for Him before you are accepted. He just loves you, and there's not one thing you can do to change that.

Make It Personal

Talk to your accountability partner or small group about your confidence or lack thereof in Jesus's love. Are you battling your past and the sins that go with it? Are you afraid and unsure? Do you lack knowledge of Scripture that can help you understand your value? If you are secure in your identity in Christ, how can you support someone who is not? Take some time to really think about how you define your identity.

_____

_____

_____

_____

_____

And So, We Pray

Dear God, You love me. Yet it can be so hard for me to understand how. As I walk with You, open my heart to know Your love. I confess that, like Hannah, I often let the world determine my value. Grow my understanding of Your love for me. Amen.

Day 6 Discussion Question

God made you unique and loves you dearly. To combat comparison, pride, and jealousy, you must know the truth about who you are in Christ. Read the following verses: John 8:36; Psalm 45:11; 2 Corinthians 5:17; and John 15:15–16. What does God say about you?

Day 7
REST AND REFLECTION

Today is a day to spend time with the Lord in any way you desire. You may choose to meditate on a Scripture from the previous week, summarize your thoughts, list your questions, or just sit quietly with the Lord. You may wish to read your Bible.

Use the space below to journal, sketch, or otherwise record your thoughts. Handwrite a Scripture or phrase. Or just take this time to sit quietly with God.

Week 3

Patience is waiting. Not passively waiting. That is laziness.
But to keep going when the going is hard and slow—
that is patience.
—Unknown

This week's journey will test your patience as you discover
why the process of waiting is so very valuable.

Day 1

How Long, O Lord?

Let us not become weary in doing good, for at the proper time we
will reap a harvest if we do not give up.
—Galatians 6:9

Today our lesson will show us that God doesn't move in
our time. We will see that patience is synonymous with long-suffering.
Hannah's story will show us how we can endure pain and difficult
circumstances over long periods while God works in and for us.

We've read 1 Samuel 1:6–7 earlier, but today we will use it to
illustrate another truth. "Because the LORD had closed Hannah's womb,
her rival kept provoking her in order to irritate her. This went on year
after year. Whenever Hannah went up to the house of the LORD, her
rival provoked her till she wept and would not eat." Use these verses to
help answer the following questions.

What did Hannah endure?

_____

Hannah was not only barren; the pain inflicted by the hands and words of another woman had broken her. Hannah's rival, Peninnah, found joy in hurting her.

How long did Hannah put up with Peninnah's torment?

Though we don't know the details, we can speculate that the provocation was repeated daily for years. These women lived, worked, and fellowshipped in close proximity.

We see in verse 7 that Hannah and her family went up to the "house of the LORD." Three times every year Hannah's husband would take the family up to the tabernacle to participate in the festivals: the Feast of Unleavened Bread, the Feast of Weeks, and the Feast of Tabernacles.

These festivals were structured times of celebration and joy in remembering what God had done for His children in the past, what He was doing in the present, and what He would do in the future. There would be special prayers, sacrifices, fellowship, reading and reciting of Scripture, and extravagant meals.

These were jubilant times for the people. But for Hannah they were especially painful. At these festivals the ache in her arms for a child, especially a son, brought her to tears. Today's Scripture evidences the depth of Hannah's pain.

Hannah wouldn't even eat. Don't you wonder why she even went to the festivals? I do. Perhaps she went out of respect for Elkanah or maybe out of a sense of obligation. Perhaps she was searching for God. We can speculate, but Scripture simply says she went.

Have you ever gone to church or Bible study even though you didn't feel like it? I have, and I absolutely hate that feeling. Sometimes our hearts just aren't in it; the pain of life's circumstances just overwhelms us and finding God is not easy.

Nevertheless, like Hannah, we have to persevere. Otherwise, if we don't at least show up, we may miss God's tender call to something better, as you will see when you read what happened next.

"Once when they had finished eating and drinking in Shiloh, Hannah stood up. Now Eli the priest was sitting on his chair by the doorpost of the LORD's house. In her deep anguish, Hannah prayed to the LORD, weeping bitterly" (1 Samuel 1:9–10).

Notice the word *once* in this passage. What did Hannah do on this one occasion?

_____

_____

_____

One time when she was at the festival, Hannah pulled herself together, slipped away quietly, and entered the sanctuary. There, she heard the call of the Lord. She allowed her brokenness to lead her to His tabernacle. After many painful years she sought and surrendered to the Lord. Oh, yeah! I know you're celebrating with me at this point. Redemption is on the way.

Hannah was growing weary, frustrated, and disillusioned. Her situation seemed hopeless. The odds were against her. She could have given up. She felt like giving up. But she didn't. She persevered. So we all have much to learn from Hannah in our desperate situations. A rough marriage. A barren womb. A wayward child. A nonbelieving spouse. A battle against cancer. The list of hurts goes on and on. But, my sweet friend, "Let us not become weary in doing good, for at the proper time we will reap a harvest if we do not give up" (Galatians 6:9).

Make It Personal

What have you been waiting on? Are you carrying the weight of hurts or fears? You need to surrender so you can receive the healing of the Lord. Are there dry, barren places in your heart that need to be filled with bountiful life? Will this moment be your "once"? Will you surrender the difficult situation, person, fear, or place of brokenness unto the Lord in exchange for His grace and tender healing?

Write a statement crying out to God and surrendering whatever you need to.

_____

_____

_____

_____

_____

_____

_____

And So, We Pray

Dear Lord, sometimes life is just very hard. My place of brokenness is real and wants to control me. But help me turn to You. Enable me to hang on when the going is rough. Lord, teach me how to persevere. Amen.

Day 1 Discussion Question

Although He could have, God did not instantly remove Hannah's pain. What might be the intended purpose of her long-suffering?

Day 2

AND STILL,
SHE WAITED

So in the course of time Hannah became pregnant and gave birth
to a son. She named him Samuel, saying,
"Because I asked the LORD for him."
—1 Samuel 1:20

After many years of hurting, Hannah went to the temple
and poured her heart out to God, asking Him for a son. First Samuel
1:10–11 reveals Hannah's heart and exposes the broken places within
her, stating:

In her deep anguish Hannah prayed to the LORD, weeping bitterly.
And she made a vow:
LORD Almighty, if you will only look on your servant's misery and
remember me, and not forget your servant but give her a son, then I
will give him to the LORD for all the days of his life, and no razor will
ever be used on his head.

Then she waited. Did God answer Hannah's prayer right away?

The phrases used in various translations to tell when Hannah bore her son, Samuel, are "so in the course of time," "in due time," and "after some time." Scripture doesn't give us the specific length of Hannah's wait, and I believe that is intentional. I believe God wants us to see that He provided in His time and not in Hannah's.

So why do you think God makes his children wait for an answer? What lessons could come from waiting?

I believe the greatest reason God makes us wait is to help us increase our perseverance in order to teach us to focus on Him. In our waiting we come to grips with our inability to fix the problem and realize we must look to God for strength and patience. Our trust must be built on the One who provides. We must continue to pour our hearts out to Him and develop our relationship with Him as we wait. We must focus on God instead of on the outcome.

What does James 1:2–3 tell us is God's reason for making us wait? "Consider it pure joy, my brothers and sisters, whenever you face trials of many kinds, because you know that the testing of your faith produces perseverance." Why doesn't He rescue us immediately from trials and struggles?

God allows our faith to be tested. He permits struggles and trials for us to develop perseverance. Waiting develops our level of commitment. However, our waiting is not only for answers to the issues of this life. We await something—Someone—greater! In biblical times the people waited for a Savior, Jesus. And since His return to heaven after His time on earth, Christians around the world eagerly wait to meet Him face-to-face at His glorious return. In the wait, God is changing us to be more and more like Him. He is preparing us for our eternal home.

God knew when Hannah was ready to receive His blessing. He knew the time in her life when she could manage it well. He met Hannah's need at the perfect time. It was exactly when He could accomplish His purposes in and through her. That's exciting, and I can't wait for you to see further how His plan unfolds in Hannah's life. If we watch carefully, we will also see God working during the wait in our lives.

I met a lady at my church years ago who had married her husband at age fifteen. She prayed for his salvation until she was eighty years old. It took sixty-five years of waiting for her prayers to be answered, but finally her husband offered his life to Jesus. The joy of her husband's salvation was worth the wait. During those years of waiting, she learned valuable life lessons. She learned to depend on God to do what she couldn't. Christ alone was her husband's Savior.

I've prayed about some matters for weeks, months, and even years. But I've also prayed about others for well over two decades. The wait may be long or short, but we can be certain God hears and answers our prayers. Sometimes He answers no. Other times He says yes. Or He may even say, "Not yet." If it appears as if God is delaying His answer, it's because He is doing a great work behind the scenes. He may be changing you. He may be changing someone else. We don't know. But we must know that He is working for our good even in the wait.

Make It Personal

If you are in a time of waiting, what lessons are you learning? Have you grown in patience and perseverance over the years? What lessons can you share with others?

_____

_____

_____

_____

_____

In what areas of your life do you need to place your focus on God more intently?

_____

_____

_____

Have you ever rushed in or forced an issue without waiting on God's timing? What happened as a result?

_____

_____

_____

_____

And So, We Pray

Dear Jesus, I can't wait to meet You face-to-face, but in the meantime I want to know You more. I want to learn to wait on You to provide for my needs and desires. I know that what You have for me is much greater than anything I could want for myself. Help me to slow down and look for Your hand and Your provision in the wait. Teach me to enjoy the process more than the outcome. Amen.

Day 2 Discussion Questions

What lessons did Hannah learn in the wait? What lessons have you learned in seasons of waiting?

Day 3
GODLY CHARACTER

But the Holy Spirit produces this kind of fruit in our lives: love,
joy, peace, patience, kindness, goodness, faithfulness, gentleness,
and self-control. There is no law against these things!
—Galatians 5:22–23 NLT

Hi, friend. As I write this chapter, I am reflecting on my
own times of waiting. I have waited for answers and mighty works from
God. Often I wanted to give up. I wanted to do things my way (not
recommended to anyone). Often I had to persevere when the pain and
desire for things to be made right were so great that I thought I couldn't
bear them.

But only by God's grace could I wait. It wasn't my own doing. His
love and strength carried me. If you were to talk to my GFFs, they would
tell you that I am not the same woman I was before. God has developed
me into a stronger woman of faith in the wait. He has shown me how
to pray through my waiting period. He has taught me how to entrust
my loved ones to Him for their healing and spiritual growth. He has

shown me that His timing is perfect. He has shown me faithfulness even when I was unfaithful.

God has met my needs, and while He was doing so, He became my desire. Praise God! Even still, He is developing godly character in me, especially as I wait on Him for answers. He wants to do the same in you.

As you read Romans 5:3–5 from your Bible, fill in the blanks of this passage:

> "Not only so, but we also glory in our sufferings, because we know that suffering produces _____ ; perseverance, _____ ; and character, _____ ."

Persevering through the wait develops godly character in us. Hanging on when we feel like giving up revives our hope. God works to use our sufferings and longings for our good. His ultimate desire is that we would become more like Him and develop a more intimate relationship with Him. Galatians 5:22–23 tells us what godly character looks like as it develops in us. Highlight the character traits in this passage:

> But the Holy Spirit produces this kind of fruit in our lives: love, joy, peace, patience, kindness, goodness, faithfulness, gentleness, and self-control. There is no law against these things!

Notice the Scripture says, "fruit of the Spirit." It's not plural (fruits) as some may believe. These nine characteristics are developed together and built upon one another simultaneously. As we grow in patience, we are also developing faithfulness. Jesus's peace in us grows as we learn to be kind and joyful in the wait. We gain self-control when we wait for God to act instead of rushing headlong into situations ahead of Him. Trust that God is doing a good thing in you as you keep on keeping on.

Make It Personal

You highlighted nine character traits that develop in the life of a Christian: love, joy, peace, patience, kindness, goodness, gentleness, faithfulness, and self-control. Honestly evaluate your own fruitfulness. Where do you see yourself lacking? As God releases His Spirit within us, we must cooperate with Him in the process of developing fruitfulness. Where is God asking you to cooperate with Him in the growing process?

_____

_____

_____

_____

_____

_____

_____

_____

And So, We Pray

Dear Lord, I ask You to develop my character. I want to be like You in all ways. Help me to look for opportunities to grow as I wait on You. You are a good, good Father. I trust that as You ask me to wait, You are working for my good. I love You. Amen.

Day 3 Discussion Question

Waiting develops godly character, which the Bible terms as the "fruit of the Spirit." What are the nine characteristics that give evidence of the spiritual growth of a Christian?

Day 4
Mature and Complete

Let perseverance finish its work so that you may be mature and
complete, not lacking anything.
—James 1:4

I am very proud of you. You're doing great. As you spend time
studying God's Word, God will reveal Himself to you in new and exciting
ways. He will change you and make you more like Him. Stay with Him.
Persevere, just as Hannah did. Let's continue seeking to understand why
God doesn't swoop in and rescue us from our circumstances. Why, like
Hannah, do we have to wait?

Hannah could have given up before she received the answer to her
prayer. She could have given up even before she started praying. She
could have allowed circumstances to determine her life story. What
would her story look like if she hadn't kept going? What if she hadn't
pushed through the pain until she found God? What if Hannah hadn't
kept going to the tabernacle year after year? What if . . . ?

Hannah's life story would have been a disaster. If she had chosen to give up, we might be reading of a woman who was destitute, bitter, and cast aside by a husband who could no longer tolerate her ugly attitude. Elkanah could have had enough of her weeping and sulking and sought a divorce.

Furthermore Hannah could have retaliated, repaid Peninnah evil for evil, and gone down in biblical history as an emotional wreck, a bitter and mean-spirited woman. Though Hannah persevered, I can't help but wonder if bitterness was Peninnah's sad life song.

However, because Hannah hung on and didn't allow her heart to become hardened and her vision jaded, she was able to grow in her faith. She was mature and complete as evidenced in verse 18: "Then she went away and ate something, and her face was no longer downcast." Through her struggles Hannah learned to trust and surrender. She found joy and peace.

In your waiting season when answers don't come quickly, when just as you seem to be getting on your feet again, a new current sweeps you under, when you begin to lose hope, remember, God is still working. He is working to make you fully dependent upon Him. He desires your whole heart. And depending on your level of pride, control, and self-righteousness, that may take some time.

A quick reflection on James 1:4—"Let perseverance finish its work so that you may be mature and complete, not lacking anything"—reminds us that waiting on God is not wasted time but, rather, is strength training.

This verse tells us that perseverance has value. Struggles and trials reveal what we are really made of in terms of our faith. As far as we can see, Hannah did not retaliate when Peninnah attacked her. Scripture doesn't paint a picture of a defiant, argumentative wife who traveled with Elkanah and her nemesis to the festival.

Hannah had every opportunity and earthly reason to be unkind or spew evil in return, but she didn't. God was developing goodness and kindness in her. Can you see the self-control it took not to lash out at Peninnah?

At the time in her life when it appeared as if Hannah was falling apart, God was behind the scenes shaping her character. In the end she would stand tall and maturely handle the blessings that He longed to bestow on her.

God entrusts trials to us not to tempt and defeat us but to test and refine our character. James 1:12 says, "Blessed is the one who perseveres under trial because, having stood the test, that person will receive the crown of life that the Lord has promised to those who love him." What is the blessing of perseverance in trials and times of waiting?

_____

_____

_____

_____

The blessing of perseverance is the crown of life, which is eternal life. Does knowing this give you a new perspective on your situation? Does knowing that God is working to make you mature and complete lift the burden of your circumstance?

God is telling us to take our eyes off the situation and focus on Him. He is beckoning us to keep striving until the day He calls us home.

Make It Personal

What has today's lesson revealed to you? How can you apply what you are learning?

_____

_____

_____

And So, We Pray

Dear Lord, help me to persevere in my faith. Connect me with others who will encourage me on this journey. Enable me to bow before You in surrender as You work to make my faith complete. Help me to persevere so that I lack nothing. Amen.

Add your own prayer, asking God to complete His master workmanship in you.

_____

_____

_____

_____

_____

_____

Day 4 Discussion Question

How does learning to wait for earthly answers benefit an individual spiritually?

Day 5
HEALING COMES

The Spirit of the Lord is on me,
because he has anointed me
to proclaim good news to the poor.
He has sent me to proclaim freedom for the prisoners
and recovery of sight for the blind,
to set the oppressed free, to proclaim the year of the Lord's favor.
—Luke 4:18–19

Some folks think we should just get over our issues and move on, and they aren't afraid to tell us so either. But not God. He always has a better plan. Every circumstance, every issue has value. As we wait and persevere, He works within us to heal our broken hearts. Read Luke 4:18–19 above. Why did God send Jesus?

_____

_____

_____

_____

Jesus came to this earth to proclaim good news to the poor, set the prisoners free, restore sight for the blind, and free the oppressed. Jesus is the healing our hearts need. He is freedom from the burdens and barrenness in our lives. Long before Hannah walked the earth, God had a plan to send Jesus as our Savior. Jesus is the healing we need for our broken and barren hearts.

Today you are going to meet another woman who found healing as she sat at the feet of Jesus. You can read the full story in Luke 7:36–50. But here is a brief synopsis.

A rich Pharisee invited Jesus to his home. Shortly after arriving at the Pharisee's home, Jesus was approached by a scandalous woman who bowed at His feet and, through streaming tears, began wiping His feet with her hair. The Pharisee, appalled that Jesus would allow such behavior from an unclean woman, began to think unkind thoughts about both Jesus and the woman.

To his dismay the Pharisee was called out for his thoughts and questioned by Jesus. A conversation ensued, yet all the while, the woman remained bowed at Jesus's feet, blessing Him and wiping His feet with perfume.

This passage introduces a woman who had spent time with Jesus prior to this scenario. She had built a friendship, trusted and loved the man who gave her new life. A man who, in a society where women were not held in high esteem, saw her broken and hurting heart. He was a man who loved her, forgave her, and expected nothing from her in return except her heart of love. He didn't use or abuse her. He adored and restored her.

This broken woman found healing through Jesus. She followed Him through the countryside. She listened to Him and let His words minister to her heart. His love overtook her. His forgiveness amazed her. And in Him she found healing.

Make It Personal

Pregnant and unwed at eighteen, I, too, have felt the deep sting of shame and rejection. Hurtful comments and disapproving glances from those I trusted and respected replayed in my heart and mind for many years. That is until the truth of Jesus's love reached deep into my heart, setting me free from the darkness of shame into the light of forgiveness.

I am so thankful that, like the woman in this story, Jesus accepted me and allowed me to remain at His feet until I was ready to stand and boldly journey on with Him.

As you walk with Jesus, He will lead you through the countryside. You will learn to hear His voice calling you and offering love and forgiveness. As you walk and talk with Him, He will minister to your heart. As you wait on Him and continue your journey, He will bring healing to the deepest places of your soul.

Wounds you thought would never heal will become scars that no longer hurt but remind you of the journey from broken to beautiful. As you wait, healing will come. Your soul will find rest even when the situation doesn't change.

And that, my friend, is a reason to praise. What can you praise the Lord for today?

And So, We Pray

Dear Lord, I am a woman at Your feet, waiting to feel Your touch and Your love. Help me to remain as You minister to the broken places in my heart. Teach me Your forgiveness and grace. Show me Your unconditional love. And as I weep, bring joy to my spirit. Amen.

Day 5 Discussion Question

The woman at the well did one thing that led her to healing. She sat at the feet of Jesus. Think about your personal quiet time. What might be your next steps in deepening your relationship with Christ?

Day 6

QUIETLY AND PATIENTLY

As she kept on praying to the LORD, Eli observed her mouth.
Hannah was praying in her heart, and her lips were moving but
her voice was not heard. Eli thought she was drunk and said to her,
"How long are you going to stay drunk? Put away your wine."
—1 Samuel 1:12–14

Ponder these words for a moment: "Hannah was praying
in her heart, and her lips were moving but her voice was not heard."
Hannah was silently praying, but God already knew her heart. It wasn't
the words of her prayer that moved the heart of God; it was the depth
of emotion in Hannah's heart and her *authenticity* that called to the
mighty One on the throne. Waiting develops relationship, and Hannah
had learned that she could talk to God when no one else understood.

My son battled an ocular tumor when he was fifteen. I begged God
to save his eye. I cried out for my son to experience a miraculous healing.

But by the time he was seventeen, the doctors had determined that removing his eye was the best way to prevent more extensive damage.

I would assume that if others had seen me praying in the quiet of my bedroom through this journey, they, too, would have thought I was a crazy drunk. My mama heart ached for my son. I cried out for God's strength and provision for my son and our family.

I spent a lot of time talking with God and reading His Word. And though the answers weren't what I wanted, the peace God offered in the wait was more than enough. God worked through our family, friends, and community to provide meals, finances, and care for our other children. God prepared every detail of my son's journey.

I begged God to spare Nicolas this surgery because I feared that others would fail to see past the physical void to the true young man beneath the surface. But God had a beautiful wife with a delightful spirit already prepared for him long before I even asked. God has made my son the strongest young man I know, and he has handled every step with grace and gratitude. He is a young man of few words, but his actions reflect a strong trust in God.

Through my times of prayer and study, God revealed Himself more fully to me. Though I would never want to walk that path again, I wouldn't trade the lessons I learned and the relationship with Jesus that I developed for anything in the world.

As we sit with Jesus, we begin to build a reciprocal relationship. We reveal ourselves to Him, and He reveals His character to us. We gain clarity into the way He thinks and acts.

As I've waited on Jesus, I've learned that He's never in a hurry. He takes time to listen. He doesn't fly off the handle when I drop a bombshell on Him about my mistakes. I've learned that I can go to Him about anything at any time.

Make It Personal

Today is set aside to sit quietly and patiently with Jesus. Read the following Scriptures. Circle one or two to meditate on today. Ask God to imprint His Word on your heart.

"Wait patiently for the LORD. Be brave and courageous. Yes, wait patiently for the LORD" (Psalm 27:14 NLT).

_____

_____

"For I am waiting for you, O LORD. You must answer me, O LORD my God" (Psalm 38:15 NLT).

_____

_____

"I waited patiently for the LORD to help me, and he turned to me and heard my cry" (Psalm 40:1 NLT).

_____

_____

"I wait quietly before God, for my victory comes from him" (Psalm 62:1 NLT).

_____

_____

"Let all that I am wait quietly before God, for my hope is in him." (Psalm 62:5 NLT).

_____

_____

"But if we hope for what we do not yet have, we wait for it patiently."
(Romans 8:25).

You may use the space provided to study the verses by rewriting or rephrasing them or making notes of thoughts that come to you as you meditate on them.

And So, We Pray

Dear Father, help me to wait patiently and quietly for You. As I study Your Word, speak to my heart. Enlighten me to Your ways. Hear my cry and answer me, for I long to know You more. Amen.

Day 6 Discussion Question

Work together with your small group to hold one another accountable for Scripture memorization between now and the next time you meet. What verse from this lesson was meaningful to you? What are some techniques you can use to commit Scripture to memory?

Day 7
Rest and Reflection

Today is a day to spend time with the Lord in any way you desire. You may choose to meditate on a Scripture from the previous week, summarize your thoughts, list your questions, or just sit quietly with the Lord. You may wish to read your Bible.

Use the space below to journal, sketch, or otherwise record your thoughts. Handwrite a Scripture or phrase. Or just take this time to sit quietly with God.

Week 4

I have a lot of respect for genuine people. They may not be perfect,
but at least they're not pretending to be.
—Anthony Gucciardi

This week you will focus on authenticity before God and others
as you learn to embrace your messes.

Day 1

HER HEART
TOUCHED MINE

"Not so, my lord," Hannah replied, "I am a woman who is deeply
troubled. I have not been drinking wine or beer;
I was pouring out my soul to the Lord."
—1 Samuel 1:15

Today you will need to carefully read 1 Samuel 1:9–20 from
your Bible. We will focus on smaller portions of this Scripture later,
but I want you to see the big picture. This space is provided so you can
take notes as you read.

_____

_____

_____

_____

This portion of Hannah's story drew me in. It's where I met Hannah and when we became friends. How could I become friends with a woman I've only met on paper? It may sound silly, but it's how I felt. Hannah had so much to teach me that I just needed to know more day after day and week after week. I had a strong desire to spend time with her. She mentored me through the misunderstandings and the weaknesses in my faith.

Let me explain. I had a faulty notion that I should have it all together as a Christian. I felt that if I had Jesus, I shouldn't have troubles, pains, or problems. As I looked around the church and among those in my small group, they all appeared to have their lives in order. No one talked about their children's mistakes, their marital struggles, or their sins. So I followed the pattern and became a part of the charade. I put on a good front too. I masked the issues in my life and walked around with a happy face. All the while, my heart didn't follow the lead of my pretense.

I struggled to find forgiveness for my past sins. I had family and work issues that I didn't talk about even among fellow Christians. Church wasn't a place where we talked about personal issues. Nor did I have an accountability partner to confide in who would give me wisdom.

However, I discovered it wasn't that others weren't talking or were hiding their truths; they just weren't opening up to me. Perhaps this was because I was quiet about my hurts and didn't appear open to others. So I tried holding myself together as best I could. From all appearances, everyone else had it all together, so why didn't I?

And then one day as I was reading my Bible, I met Hannah in front of the temple. She was there, crying out to God, her body bent in prayer upon the steps. I could see her. Her dress was draping her worn and weary body. I saw her head bowed and her arms raised to heaven. As I read her story, I could vividly see the anguish on her face as tears flowed from her eyes and her lips trembled.

I was compelled to let my tears flow as I envisioned hers falling from her eyes. I was touched by the way she exposed her heart—the good, bad, and ugly—to God right there on the temple steps. Hannah's mouth was moving as I watched her talk to the Lord, yet no words escaped her lips. Her heart was pouring out to the only One who could help her. She wasn't worried about what everyone else saw or how they might perceive her. She was seeking God with abandon.

It was the most beautiful sight I had ever seen. Then I was shocked when Eli the chief priest approached her, asking if she'd been drinking. Admittedly she did look like a crazy woman. Nevertheless she simply responded, "I am a woman who is deeply troubled. I have not been drinking wine or beer; I was pouring out my soul to the LORD" (1 Samuel 1:15). Those words spoke to the depths of my heart. I fell in love with her God, who heard her prayer and loved her despite her shortcomings and her mess.

Hannah inspired me to get real with God. She showed me how to lie on my bedroom floor and pour out my heart. She showed me that it was okay to want something more from this life. Hannah's story gave me permission to be authentic with God.

Dear friend, I pray you will let God use Hannah's story to transform your relationship with Him and others.

Make It Personal

Is it easy for you to share your heart openly with God?

Do you feel He knows you intimately because you've talked to Him about every aspect of your life?

If not, what do you feel keeps you from being open and honest with Him?

_____

_____

_____

A good way to gauge your ability to open up to God is to assess how easily you can open up to other people. If you are guarded with others, you are most likely guarding your heart from God. Reread 1 Samuel 1:1–20 and watch as Hannah shows you how to get real with God.

Do you see anything new today about Hannah's relationship with God that you can apply to your life?

_____

_____

_____

And So, We Pray

Dear God, I pray today that You open my eyes to see the truths in Hannah's story. Show me how to open up and be free to live in this kind of relationship with You. As I reread her story, enlighten me so I can see her intimate relationship with You and have the courage to move into a deeper relationship with You also. Amen.

Day 1 Discussion Question

Hannah's heart was raw and open before the Lord, but she wasn't always able to talk with Him authentically. It was a journey. Where are you on this journey of authenticity with God? Rate yourself on a scale of zero to five, with zero meaning this is all new to you and five meaning you are free to bare your soul to Him.

Day 2
AUTHENTIC PRAYER

And when you pray, do not be like the hypocrites, for they love to
pray standing in the synagogues and on the street corners to be seen
by others. Truly I tell you, they have received their reward in full.
But when you pray, go into your room, close the door and pray
to your Father, who is unseen. Then your Father, who sees what is
done in secret, will reward you. And when you pray, do not keep
on babbling like pagans, for they think they will be heard because
of their many words. Do not be like them, for your Father knows
what you need before you ask him.
—Matthew 6:5–8

Yesterday we saw how Hannah spoke with God at the temple
steps. She prayed in her anguish with tears. She prayed in the presence
of the priest and others. She prayed with honesty and commitment.
Hannah's openness before God is beautiful. She wasn't worried about
what others thought. She was only concerned about her conversation
with God as she bared her broken heart before Him.

Jesus has much to say about praying in today's passage. As you read Matthew 6:5–8, highlight the phrases that teach you how to pray and things to avoid when praying.

Note the phrases within this Scripture that will help you pray so God will honor your prayers.

_____

_____

_____

_____

_____

What phrases represent prayers of a hypocrite?

_____

_____

_____

_____

Hannah was not a hypocrite like those referred to in this passage. She was sincere. She prayed knowing God heard her heart. She wasn't putting on a show for others to see. She wasn't using fancy words or trying to impress those who passed by on their way to the temple.

She totally focused on God. So much so that she wasn't even aware that others were watching. She was simply baring her heart to the One who loved her and knew her life was messy. And her authentic prayer was stunningly beautiful to the heart of her God.

Make It Personal

I can remember a time when I was afraid to pray in front of anyone other than my children. If anyone ever asked for prayer, I would look away in hopes that they would pass over me to someone who was better at prayer than I was. Can you relate? If so, why do you think you are afraid to pray in the presence of others?

_____

_____

_____

I was worried I would stutter or say something silly. I was more concerned with what others would think than with what I was saying to God. And then God used Hannah's story to change my heart. Hannah reminded me that prayer was just between God and me. She reminded me that He wanted my heart, not just my words. And the only way to overcome my fear of praying was to do it more often in the quiet of my bedroom.

I could practice opening up to God and trusting that He saw my heart even when my words were messy. And you know what? He did! The more time I spent alone with God, the more I had the freedom to open up to others. I learned that I can pray in the quietness of my heart, openly in the presence of others, in long sittings or fleeting moments.

Through Hannah, God opened my heart to an amazing, never-ending dialogue with Him, and He wants to do the same with you.

And So, We Pray

Dear Lord, teach me to pray as You have illustrated through Your Word. Open my heart to deep, rich conversations with You. Remove the barriers of fear and pride from my heart and mind so I can freely commune with You. Pour Your Holy Spirit out upon me and lead me in the way You want me to go, directing me through prayer.

In Your precious name, sweet Jesus, I pray. Amen.

Day 2 Discussion Question

Hannah prayed openly before God and others. Prayer is simply a conversation with God. However, public prayer can be difficult.

Is prayer an area you and your study group might focus on in the future?

Day 3

COURAGEOUS TRANSPARENCY

Not that I have already obtained all this, or have already arrived at my goal, but I press on to take hold of that for which Christ Jesus took hold of me. Brothers and sisters, I do not consider myself yet to have taken hold of it. But one thing I do: Forgetting what is behind and straining toward what is ahead, I press on toward the goal to win the prize for which God has called me heavenward in Christ Jesus.

—Philippians 3:12–14

If you are going to work at being authentic, you must address the issue of courage. Hannah was once broken, but as her story draws to an end, she stands bold and beautiful. That transformation didn't take place without courage to acknowledge the hurt and brokenness in her life. Courage to be real. Courage to be vulnerable.

Her transformation required countless moments of prayer with God, painful self-reflection, and no doubt much conversation with

Elkanah and perhaps other women in her village. Hannah had to come face-to-face with who she was in order to discover who she was meant to be. She had to embrace her inadequacies to discover the redeeming power of God. Hannah is not the only one from Scripture who can guide us in authentic living.

As I mentioned earlier in the study, the apostle Paul was the greatest evangelist to ever walk this earth. Yet he was not without flaws, failures, and fears. He shared them openly with those he ministered to, and because of his authenticity, others were drawn to him. They could relate to his humanness and in turn wrestle with their own fallibility as they sought to follow a holy, perfect God.

In today's Scripture Paul shares that his life is still messy. He doesn't have it all together, but that did not diminish his understanding of God's grace and goodness. It actually empowered his message, giving it merit. Paul's ability to embrace his challenges and shortcomings allowed him to be vulnerable with God and others, a courageous state to live in.

Make It Personal

Over the last few years, I have been much more open about my trials, temptations, and tears. The first time I shared portions of my messes, I was scared of rejection and the oh-dear expression that I expected in response.

But what I found was that transparency was actually a bridge that allowed others to share their stories and find healing as well.

Where do you need to be more vulnerable? What barriers keep you from being authentic and living transparently?

_____

_____

_____

_____

_____

_____

_____

_____

And So, We Pray

Use the space below to share your heart with the Lord. Tell Him what is on your mind—freely, confidently, honestly.

Girlfriend, be courageously transparent.

_____

_____

_____

_____

_____

Day 3 Discussion Question

Transparency takes courage, a courage not found in your strengths but in your ability to let your weaknesses be used by God. What is one trial, temptation, or tear that you can share your group? Remember, your transparency frees others to be vulnerable with themselves, you, and God.

Day 4

It's Okay to Be Honest

Cast all your anxiety on him because he cares for you.
—1 Peter 5:7

Hannah struggled in her private pain. She crumbled under the torment and ached through the circumstances in her own strength for years. Remember that "once" Hannah decided to deal with her issue. "Once" she decided to lay it out honestly before God. I often wonder how many people in the world need a "once" moment.

I see angry, bitter, tired people all the time. Yes, even in the church. I see people who wear masks over their faces so others won't know what's really going on in their spirits. And I see others who are depressed, angry, or anxious every day.

I believe those people need a "once" in their lives. They need to allow God to break down the walls that have been created around their hearts so they can be honest with Him. As I shared earlier in the study, I have been that girl, the one hidden behind a mask of perfection, though I was broken and afraid. I was the one struggling with depression and fear. I too carried burdens I didn't need to bear alone.

Hannah carried her burden year after year. She wept and was weary. Her husband, Elkanah, would say to her, "Hannah, why are you weeping? Why don't you eat? Why are you downhearted? Don't I mean more to you than ten sons?" (1 Samuel 1:8).

Bless his heart! Elkanah gave Hannah a double portion of his blessing and the abundance of his love. He reassured her that, just as she was, she was enough. He offered her his encouragement, but it did not meet her deepest needs. Hannah needed the healing that only God could bring, the healing that touches the deep crevices of the soul. And "once" she poured the ugliness, pain, and desires of her heart out, letting God fill her with His truth and love.

Hannah did just what God wants us to do. First Peter 5:7—"Cast all your anxiety on him because he cares for you"—gives us guidance on how to handle our cares and concerns.

The word *cast* literally means to throw. Here Scripture is telling us to throw our concerns to Jesus. I don't envision throwing them gently. Put some weight behind your throw. You will discover that God doesn't want us to come to Him only when our emotions are controlled and intact. He doesn't want us to tiptoe around our true feelings. He wants honest, gut-wrenching, sincere conversation.

He's strong enough to deal with our anger. His shoulders are mighty enough to take our bitterness and negative emotions. He understands our fears and wants to relieve them. And He is tender enough to gently deal with our hurts and brokenness.

Look up these passages. How did the author of each speak to the Lord?

Psalm 62:8 _____

Psalm 142:1–2 _____

Psalm 130:1 _____

These writers poured out and cried out. They honestly revealed what was going on in their hearts and minds to the One who could do something about their problems.

Make It Personal

Did you know you could tell God you are angry? Did you know you could tell Him how badly you wish the circumstances were different? Did you know He's not mad at you because you feel a certain way? Did you know you could be honest? Well, you can. And He's waiting for you to do so.

He is not obligated to change your circumstances or give you the answers you want. However, because He is sovereign, He has your best interest in mind. He allows you to be real with Him about your feelings because being real permits Him to heal and change you.

And So, We Pray

Dear Lord, help me deal with the messes in my life rather than close them off by avoiding them, stuffing them down, or building walls around them. Lord, help me to throw my bitterness and anger on You. Help me to deal with any hurt, fear, anger, or discouragement in my heart. Help me to deal with insecurity or jealousy.

Give me the courage to face my pride or lack of commitment. Lord, help me to deal with _____.
Show me how to be in real relationship with You. Amen.

Day 4 Discussion Questions

Many people feel they cannot express anger, fear, or other negative emotions to God when they are hurting. But Hannah shows us that honesty about our messes is highly honored by God. Does this concept surprise you? Why or why not?

Day 5

MESSES
BECOME GLORY

Early the next morning they arose and worshiped before the Lord
and then went back to their home at Ramah. Elkanah made love to
his wife Hannah, and the Lord remembered her. So in the course of
time Hannah became pregnant and gave birth to a son. She named
him Samuel, saying, "Because I asked the Lord for him."
—1 Samuel 1:19–20

Today we will celebrate God's glory. I love this part, and I
believe you will too. As you read 1 Samuel 1:19–20, look for displays
of God's glory. List any observances here:

_____

_____

_____

Elkanah made love to his wife; she became pregnant and bore a son. And the beauty is that Hannah gave God all the glory. She revealed her heart of love for God when she gave God all the glory for His work in her life. Even the child's name, Samuel, reflects God's glory. What does the name Samuel mean (v. 20)?

God didn't just give Hannah a son. Samuel was dedicated to the Lord and became one of Israel's greatest prophets. God's glory had captivated Hannah's heart, and He knew she would be faithful to the call He had on her life. God is not obligated to answer your prayers as you would like, but He will always hear, respond, and work for your best interest, just as He did for Hannah.

Your messes cannot separate you from the love of God, though it is easy to give them the power to keep you from being honest and real with Him. When hurts run deep, or shame and guilt plague your heart, it is easy to shut God out instead of allowing the authenticity of our situation to be an opening for God to get into our hearts long enough to bring healing.

Our hurts are raw, and any touch seems painful. Yet if you allow the Word of God to minister to your pain, you will find the healing balm you so desperately need. God is a master surgeon, peeling back one layer of tissue, one small issue at a time, until He has dealt with every messy, hurting place in your heart.

Psalm 139:16 says of God, "Your eyes saw my unformed body; all the days ordained for me were written in your book before one of them came to be."

All the days of your life were written in God's book. He knows everything about the past, present, and future of your life. You need to know that a glorious mess doesn't surprise God. It does not shock or intimidate Him. Heaven isn't rattled when your personal world is shaken. God already knows how you feel, but He wants you to talk to Him about it.

So, like Hannah, the next step is to talk to Him when those situations arise. He waits for you to trust Him. He waits for you to open up to Him. He isn't mad at you. He isn't going to say, I told you so. Your messed-up situations and messed-up life provide opportunities for personal change and deepened faith.

Perhaps you are in a refining fire, a fire that is burning off impurities and flaws in your faith. The fiery process of refinement makes you better, stronger, and more beautiful.

These trials will show that your faith is genuine. It is being tested as fire tests and purifies gold—though your faith is far more precious than mere gold. So when your faith remains strong through many trials, it will bring you much praise and glory and honor on the day when Jesus Christ is revealed to the whole world (1 Peter 1:7 NLT).

Through trials those who have surface faith may give up and turn from God because the fire gets hotter, the pains go deeper, and the consequences become greater. A choice has to be made. You can turn from God and live in the chaos or turn to God and allow Him to do what only He can do to redeem our messes.

Make It Personal

Whether you are a new Christian or a longtime follower of Christ, messes are bound to be part of your life. Take time to sit quietly with God today and reflect on His glory.

Where have you seen God work in your messiness? How have you matured in your faith because of the mistakes or trials you've faced?

If you committed an issue to Him during your quiet time yesterday, what are your next steps in allowing Him to work in you?

_____

_____

_____

_____

_____

_____

And So, We Pray

Heavenly Father, I ask that You change my messes to Your glory. I ask for Your help in allowing the trials, mistakes, and confusion in my life to be lessons for maturing my faith. Refine me in the fire of Your goodness. Strengthen my weak faith, and let Your name be honored and praised because of the work You've done through my messes. Amen.

Day 5 Discussion Question

What new truths are you learning about the messy places of your life?

Day 6

The Weak
Made Strong

But he said to me, "My grace is sufficient for you, for my power is
made perfect in weakness." Therefore I will boast all the more gladly
about my weaknesses, so that Christ's power may rest on me.
—2 Corinthians 12:9

One would expect Hannah to be the loser in this story.
She was weak, and by the standards of our world, the weak don't stand
a chance. Peninnah was fierce, and Hannah had no way of changing the
barrenness of her womb on her own. By all earthly accounts it would
seem that Hannah was defeated.

But God isn't like the world. He doesn't think like the world. "'For
my thoughts are not your thoughts, neither are your ways my ways,'
declares the LORD" (Isaiah 55:8).

What does God do for the weak, as stated in Isaiah 40:29?

_____

_____

_____

Yes! "He gives strength to the weary and increases the power of the weak."

Read 1 Corinthians 1:26–28.

> Brothers and sisters, think of what you were when you were called. Not many of you were wise by human standards; not many were influential; not many were of noble birth. But God chose the foolish things of the world to shame the wise; God chose the weak things of the world to shame the strong. God chose the lowly things of this world and the despised things—and the things that are not—to nullify the things that are.

How do God's thoughts differ from human thoughts as described in these verses?

_____

_____

_____

_____

_____

_____

God does not see as the world sees. In fact, His ways are often the exact opposite of the world's. God saw value and beauty in Hannah and her situation. Her weakness would proclaim His strength.

You may be ashamed of your weaknesses. But Paul, the most influential man ever to share the gospel of Jesus, learned to view his weaknesses as assets.

In 2 Corinthians 12:9, Paul says, "But he said to me, 'My grace is sufficient for you, for my power is made perfect in weakness.' Therefore I will boast all the more gladly about my weaknesses, so that Christ's power may rest on me."

Why should we adopt Paul's way of thinking?

_____

_____

_____

When you are weak, the world around you knows it. They will also notice when you overcome situations that should have squashed you under their weight. That's when Christ's glory shines through. He is magnified, and you stand on His strength just like Hannah.

Make It Personal

It's not easy to admit your weaknesses and your mistakes, but admission is a key step to deliverance. Today spend a few moments examining yourself. Be honest, even when it's hard to face the truth.

First be honest with yourself, and then talk with God. You will find freedom in admitting your mistakes, fears, feelings, and hurts. God is not going to condemn you.

Remember He longs for you to talk openly with Him and to develop a closer relationship with Him. He will not punish you or be disappointed in you. Through your weaknesses, Christ will be glorified. So now, go on and get to it. Share your heart with God.

_____

_____

_____

_____

_____

_____

_____

_____

_____

And So, We Pray

Dear Lord, I pray that You will open my heart and eyes to see my weaknesses. I want Your power to rest on me. As I learn to be more open with You and others, I pray I will not be ashamed of my weaknesses. I will let Your strength shine through me in those areas. Amen.

Day 6 Discussion Question

Hannah's situation left her broken. She was powerless to change on her own. But God does not view weaknesses as the world views them. How does God view and use our weaknesses for His purposes?

Day 7
Rest and Reflection

Today is a day to spend time with the Lord in any way you desire. You may choose to meditate on a Scripture from the previous week, summarize your thoughts, list your questions, or just sit quietly with the Lord. You may wish to read your Bible.

Use the space below to journal, sketch, or otherwise record your thoughts. Handwrite a Scripture or phrase. Or just take this time to sit quietly with God.

To pray is to let go and let God take over.
—Philippians 4:6–7 (author paraphrase)

This week you will focus on how to worship God as you entrust
Him with your wounds, fears, and desires.

Day 1

LET GO

Let us then approach God's throne of grace with confidence, so that
we may receive mercy and find grace to help us in our time of need.
—Hebrews 4:16

This week our focus shifts to Hannah's surrender. We will see
the beautiful way she handed over her requests to God and waited for
Him to answer. And we will be blessed by what she did as she waited for
God to act. Through Hannah's story I pray you will also gain confidence
and strength. Let's not waste another moment to discover these truths.

We've already looked at how Hannah went to the temple and poured
out her heart honestly to the Lord. Remember how she was so caught
up in her dialogue with God that the priest perceived her to be drunk?
But Hannah wasn't drunk at all; not one drop had touched her lips. She
was being real and baring her heart before the Lord.

Today you will look at God's Word and unveil Scripture that will
encourage and empower you to approach God confidently, even in your
weaknesses, just like Hannah.

Use Hebrews 4:16 to answer the questions: "Let us then approach God's throne of grace with confidence, so that we may receive mercy and find grace to help us in our time of need."

How should we approach God's throne?

_____

_____

_____

_____

What should we expect to find when we open our hearts to Him?

_____

_____

_____

_____

When should we go to God?

_____

_____

_____

_____

God is available 24-7, always ready and waiting to help us with anything that is in our hearts. This Scripture, this truth of God, tells us we can go to Him in our times of need without shame or fear, and God will not mock us because of our failures and inadequacies. He may discipline us if we have wandered from His will, but all discipline will be done with mercy and grace.

Therefore we go confidently, knowing He is ready to help us. Don't you just love that? Doesn't that make you feel safe and secure? It sure makes me feel that way; I can just curl up on His big daddy lap and share whatever, whenever. That love is out of this world. That is love you can trust.

Ephesians 3:12—"In him and through faith in him we may approach God with freedom and confidence"—tells us more about approaching God.

What should we feel besides confidence when we go to God? Freedom. No bondage. No shame. No regrets. No fear. Just freedom.

Make It Personal

As a young Christian I feared talking to God. I was afraid of saying the wrong words, uncomfortable with being honest about my feelings, and often ashamed of my choices. My common response was to simply not talk to God. However, I've learned that God's not shocked by my feelings, He's not caught up by my lack of words, and He has always traded my shame for grace. My journey with God has brought freedom and authenticity to our relationship.

How about you? Do you feel free to talk to God?

_____

_____

What emotions do you have as you contemplate talking with the Lord?

_____

_____

_____

Use this space to express your needs or thoughts today.

_____

_____

_____

_____

_____

And So, We Pray

Dear Heavenly Father, help me to approach Your throne with confidence. Not that I would have confidence in myself or in my situation, but confidence that You are ready to receive and help me in my time of need. God, Your Word says I can come freely, so give me courage to be open and honest with You. I love You for loving me so very much. Amen.

Day 1 Discussion Question

I find it interesting that Hannah confidently approached the throne of God, yet as she did she was sprawled out in tears at the temple steps. This is not an earthly image of confidence. How does confidence in God differ from confidence as expressed in our culture?

Day 2
GO ON YOUR WAY

She said, "May your servant find favor in your eyes." Then she
went her way and ate something, and her face was no longer
downcast. Early the next morning they arose and worshiped before
the Lord and then went back to their home at Ramah. Elkanah
made love to his wife Hannah, and the Lord remembered her.
—1 Samuel 1:18–19

Yesterday we saw how Hannah laid down her struggles. But
what do you do after you lay your requests at the feet of God?

Read 1 Samuel 1:18–19 again. What did Hannah do when she was
finished praying?

_____

_____

_____

The Scripture simply says, "She went on her way and ate something."
Hannah got up and got back to business. She knew God had heard her,

and that was all she needed. She knew God loved her and would not ignore her. But to get back to business, she had to make a few details absolutely clear in her heart and mind.

First, she had to establish that God is sovereign. That means God is in absolute control. Nothing happens without His permission or His direction. He has a plan that cannot be thwarted. Hannah had to believe that either sovereign God would give her a son or He would sustain her if she remained barren. Either way, it was in His hands.

"We have also received an inheritance in Christ. We were destined by the plan of God, who accomplishes everything according to his design" (Ephesians 1:11 CEB).

In Christ, God had a plan long before we were born. He will accomplish everything in that plan. His plan is for you to be with Him in heaven. Circumstances on this earth don't define you; they refine you.

The situations you face are preparing and fine-tuning you to be fit for His kingdom. Keep your eyes up and focused on eternity. For Hannah to trust God's sovereignty, she had to look up and focus on Him, not on her situation.

Read Isaiah 14:24. What does God say He will do with His plans?

_____

_____

_____

God will do what He set out to do. His word is good. So trust in it confidently.

Second, Hannah had to learn to rely fully on God. For the following verse, I've opted to use the New Living Translation because it clearly states that our struggles are not without purpose.

"We are pressed on every side by troubles, but we are not crushed. We are perplexed, but not driven to despair. We are hunted down, but never abandoned by God. We get knocked down, but we are not destroyed" (2 Corinthians 4:8–9 NLT).

Paul, the writer of this passage, suffered great persecution for sharing the message of Christ. He was imprisoned, shipwrecked three times, beaten, stoned, threatened, sleepless, hungry, and cold. Yet he recalls these events to remind us that through every circumstance, God was faithful. God doesn't waste anything in our lives. He uses both the good and the bad to spread the message of His faithfulness and redeeming love. Not only did God's faithfulness permeate Paul's circumstances, through them, Paul himself became a mighty man of faith. He grew in the character of God.

Just when Hannah was at her end, God was waiting to carry her. Her weakness became His strength. He waited patiently for her to hand her life over to Him. Paul's story was the same. Mine is too. Do you see the common thread?

Difficult circumstances, trials, and the pressures of life will weigh us down, but God is waiting to shoulder the weight. His love is patient and strong. And Hannah would embody these same characteristics as she learned to rely fully on God.

Make It Personal

Have you settled the matters of sovereignty and reliance in your heart and mind? Do you truly believe God is sovereign? Do you believe He has a plan for you and He will carry it out? Have you learned to rely fully on God? The trial or issue you face (or the one that may come in the future) has already been taken care of by God. Don't worry that you are still learning to rely more fully on God. He eagerly awaits the journey with you.

What do you need Him to make clear to you so you can more fully rely on His faithful character? What have you learned from Paul and Hannah's stories?

Paul's words from 2 Corinthians 4 tell us that through the messes, we can learn to rely on God to sustain us. Some choose to rely on themselves, a pill, a bottle, or a certain way of life. But blessed are those who, like Paul and Hannah, can turn their hearts and minds to the Lord.

And So, We Pray

Today pray specifically, asking God to help you grow to understand His sovereignty. Ask Him to enable you to depend fully on Him as you continue in faith. You may wish to record your prayer here.

Day 2 Discussion Question

Hannah's faith journey took years. Even after her surrender at the temple steps, we can be sure she had bouts of self-reliance and moments of doubt. Can you relate? Explain.

Day 3

LET GOD

This resurrection life you received from God is not a timid,
grave-tending life. It's adventurously expectant, greeting God with
a childlike "What's next, Papa?" God's Spirit touches our spirits
and confirms who we really are. We know who he is, and we know
who we are: Father and children. And we know we are going to get
what's coming to us—an unbelievable inheritance! We go through
exactly what Christ goes through. If we go through the hard times
with him, then we're certainly going to go through the good times
with him!

—Romans 8:15–17 MSG

Though God had not yet revealed His answer to Hannah, she
went about her business knowing God would meet her needs. God is
a good Father, preparing what His children need before they even ask.

I remember when my children were small and would begin fussing
and look to me for help. I knew if they needed a nap, a snack, or just a
cuddle to bring them back to a place of contentment. They didn't have

to ask; my mama heart just knew what they needed because I knew them better than anyone.

God knows us even more intimately. Hannah had to learn to let go so God could do what only He could do in her and for her.

Romans 8:15–17 tells us that upon receiving God's Spirit, we are made His children. He adopts us as His own. In biblical times an adoption was irrevocable. As a customary Roman practice of the time, a person could disown his biological children, but he could never disown an adopted child.[1] Paul's statement in Romans 8:15–17 signifies this truth. We are God's forever. Knowing this truth frees us to cry out to Him because he is our Daddy.

We are told throughout Scripture that our Father God will meet all our needs. What is your image/perception of a father?

_____

_____

_____

_____

I'd be foolish to believe that everyone has a positive, safe, and happy perception of a father. I want you to know that whatever your perception is, God is better. He is the perfect father.

Read Psalm 33:5. "The LORD loves righteousness and justice; the earth is full of his unfailing love."

---

[1] https://aleteia.org/2017/09/12/how-the-roman-practice-of-adoption-sheds-light-on-what-st-paul-was-talking-about/.

How is God's love described?

_____

_____

_____

We've all been disappointed, let down, and betrayed by others. But God's love is unfailing. Yes, circumstances may leave us feeling less than loved, but the truth is that God won't let us down.

Read Philippians 4:19. "And my God will meet all your needs according to the riches of his glory in Christ Jesus."

From where will God supply all your needs?

_____

_____

_____

God longs to give you His best. From His glorious riches, which we receive through Christ's death and resurrection, He will meet your needs.

So you see, dear friend, Hannah could go about her business with joy in her heart because she knew her Daddy was in charge. She realized He only wanted to give her blessings from His glorious stockpile of amazing gifts. She let go and let God do what only He could do.

Hannah did not know God would give her a son, but she rested in His love and grace. And that was the fulfillment she needed more than she needed a son.

Make It Personal

What do you need today? Talk to God about your needs.

_____

_____

_____

_____

_____

_____

_____

_____

And So, We Pray

Dear Lord, help me to know You as my Papa. As I walk and talk with You, open my heart and eyes to see Your goodness. I want to let go and let You do what's best for me. Teach my heart the art of surrender. Amen.

Day 3 Discussion Question

What do you think it means when Scripture says God wants to give to us from His glorious riches?

Day 4
Joy in the Trial

Peace I leave with you; my peace I give you.
I do not give to you as the world gives.
Do not let your hearts be troubled and do not be afraid.
—John 14:27

Hannah learned to let go and trust God to do what He wanted to do. And she did it with a joyful heart. First Samuel 1:18 tells us, "Her face was no longer downcast." Just when Hannah had lost all hope of having a child, she let go and found the true source of hope, a God who loved her and pursued her relentlessly.

But God loved her too much to give her the greatest desire of her heart before He became the greatest desire of her heart. So, at just the right time, Hannah opened her heart to the Lord, and He rushed in to capture His rightful place as Lord of her life.

She entered the temple hopeless and desperate, yet Hannah arose from her place on the steps and left with joy and peace.

Joy, peace? Yes, joy and peace. Hannah possessed a deep inner peace and contentment despite the difficulty around her.

So where do you find this kind of joy in your glorious mess? Where do you find this peace despite the chaos that encircles you?

Read the words of Jesus found in John 14:27: "Peace I leave with you; my peace I give you. I do not give to you as the world gives. Do not let your hearts be troubled and do not be afraid."

Our peace comes from Jesus's peace. And Jesus's peace comes from God the Father. You see, Jesus isn't worried about anything because He knows His Father will never fail. Jesus knows God the Father has a plan for good. We can have peace because our faith in Jesus is directly linked to God's faithfulness.

Hannah chose to get up and leave her place of prayer with joy in her heart. Friend, I encourage you to choose to live joyfully because this life isn't the end. It isn't the best it gets. Heaven awaits you, and that, my dear friend, should make your heart sing.

Today just mull these verses over and over in your mind. Allow them to penetrate the deeper places of your heart.

"We're depending on God; he's everything we need. What's more, our hearts brim with joy since we've taken for our own his holy name. Love us, God, with all you've got—that's what we're depending on" (Psalm 33:20–22 MSG).

This verse says nothing about getting all we want in this life on earth. But what we do get is the joy of knowing God loves us with all He's got and that we are assured of the promise of heaven, where pain, doubt, fear, and all life's other negatives do not exist.

Make It Personal

I can tell you from personal experience that if you are waiting for a situation to change to be joyful, you are wasting a lot of time. You are loved right where you are today. Dig deeper into your relationship with Christ to experience true freedom and joy.

What is stealing your joy? Have you lost hope because you are trusting in something or someone other than Christ? Has your pain become your focus? If so, make a conscious choice to praise God for His faithfulness and love. Praise is a mysterious act that releases joy even in the midst of the most painful circumstances.

And So, We Pray

Dear Father, I confess that I have placed my hope in people and things that have only led to disappointment. I want to experience the true joy and freedom of living in Your love. Your love came at the cost of Your Son's life on the cross. Christ died that I may experience the joy of Your salvation. Teach me to live like Hannah did—joyfully, despite my circumstances, fears, failures, and every other attempt to steal my joy. You alone are my joy. Amen.

Add your own prayer acknowledging your need for Christ as your joy.

_____

_____

_____

_____

_____

_____

_____

Day 4 Discussion Question

Discuss John 14:27. What is meant by Jesus's statement, "I give you my peace"?

Day 5
Worship Him

Then my head will be exalted above the enemies who surround me;
at his sacred tent I will sacrifice with shouts of joy; I will sing and
make music to the Lord.
—Psalm 27:6

Yesterday we saw how Hannah traded her downcast spirit for a spirit of joy. She took her eyes off the situation and put them on the Lord. Rather than focus on how and when He would answer, Hannah rested in the fact that He had heard her. God alone became her joy. Repeatedly in God's Word we can see how joy manifests itself.

In the following verses, how do you see the writers expressing joy?

1 Chronicles 16:33 _____

Nehemiah 12:43 _____

Psalm 20:5 _____

Psalm 27:6 _____

Psalm 28:7 _____

When joy comes to our hearts, it has to find a way out. It expresses itself through worship. Worship, as pointed out through these verses, is done in the form of words of praise, singing, leaping, and rejoicing. Worship isn't characterized simply as a church service on Sunday morning or a devotional time: rather it is a way of life. Joy manifests itself in various ways, but it begins with a decision, a choice to focus on the blessings of life in Christ rather than the disappointments and hurts.

Make It Personal

Are you joyful? Highlight your current ranking on the joy meter below:

0—If I can just get through this next moment/day/week, maybe I'll feel joyful.
1—I'm not joyful, but I'm making it.
2—I'm learning to let go, but it's still such a struggle.
3—I feel my joy in the Lord growing every day, slowly but steadily.
4—I'm mostly joyful, but once in a while I take my eyes off the Lord.
5—I'm overflowing with joy. It bursts out of me and flows onto those around me.

Good news! God is pleased with your honesty. You may have ranked yourself as a zero on the joy meter, or you may have ranked yourself a five. Whichever the case, God wants to meet you right where you are. Keep reading His Word. Continue talking with others. Grow in your prayer time with Jesus. You're doing great.

What is your next step in seeking the Lord, worshiping Him, and living in His joy?

_____

_____

_____

_____

And So, We Pray

Today, write your own prayer. Share whatever is on your heart with the Lord.

_____

_____

_____

_____

_____

_____

_____

_____

_____

Day 5 Discussion Question

Talk about your ranking on the joy meter. What might cause you to be more joyful?

Day 6

EXCHANGE WITH EXPECTATION

"The young women will dance and be glad, young men and old
as well. I will turn their mourning into gladness; I will give them
comfort and joy instead of sorrow. I will satisfy the priests with
abundance, and my people will be filled with my bounty,"
declares the Lord.
—Jeremiah 31:13–14

Yesterday we saw Hannah find joy. She gave herself to
God and received something in exchange. You may wonder what you
have to offer God that is of any value.

But the truth is you will be surprised at what He really wants from
you. He wants all the "yuck." He wants your sorrows and mistakes. He
wants your sordid past and your fears. He wants the hurt that others
spewed on you. He wants the worst of you in exchange for the best of
Him.

This, my friend, is called grace. You can't earn it. You can't buy it. It is simply a gift that is given to you out of unfathomable love. God longs to lavish His grace on you, and when you begin to internalize the fact that His love has overcome your adversity, those around you will take notice and say, "Girl, grace looks good on you."

Let's take a look at this truth in Scripture.

Read Jeremiah 31:13. What does God give us in exchange for our mourning and sorrow?

Hannah exchanged her sorrow for joy. She gave up her pain for His healing. She offered God the ugliness of her life, and He filled her with His hope and joy. The good news about trading with God is that it's never an even exchange; He always throws in a free upgrade. We give Him our junk, and He gives us His glory.

As you learn to lay your requests honestly before the Lord, you can leave your place of prayer in joy. After reading the following verses, explain how you should offer Him your requests and what you can expect in return.

"Hear my cry for help, my King and my God, for to you I pray. In the morning, LORD, you hear my voice; in the morning I lay my requests before you and wait expectantly" (Psalm 5:2–3).

"I waited patiently for the LORD; he turned to me and heard my cry. He lifted me out of the slimy pit, out of the mud and mire; he set my feet on a rock and gave me a firm place to stand" (Psalm 40:1–2).

_____

_____

_____

We are to lay our requests before the Lord in expectation, knowing He will answer. He may not answer as we would like or as quickly as we want, but we can wait expectantly, knowing He is faithful to answer in His way and His time for our good. Deuteronomy 7:9 is our confirmation that God was, is, and will continue to be faithful: "Know therefore that the LORD your God is God; he is the faithful God, keeping his covenant of love to a thousand generations of those who love him and keep his commandments."

Make It Personal

More than once I've had to offer God what I dearly loved in exchange for His strength, grace, and provision. I've offered Him my husband and son as they battled cancer in exchange for the assurance of His healing both spiritual and physical.

I've offered him my daughters, when their hearts were shattered by the selfishness of another, in exchange for His strength and provision.

I've offered Him my marriage in exchange for His love and patience. And I've given Him myself, when I'd fallen into the darkness of depression, in exchange for the light of His presence.

What do you offer God today in expectation, knowing He has heard your prayer and will answer you in His time and in His way?

_____

_____

_____

_____

_____

_____

_____

_____

And So, We Pray

Dear Lord, today I'm exchanging my junk for Your glory. Help me to surrender my pain, fear, bitterness, indifference, unforgiveness, and/ or _____.

God, I lay this down with eager expectation that You have heard me and will answer. Nourish my heart as I wait. Make me patient by asking me to be patient. Teach me Your faithfulness by teaching me to be faithful to You. Teach me the process of surrendering to You each day. Amen.

Day 6 Discussion Question

What are your thoughts about exchanging your junk for God's glory?

Day 7
REST AND REFLECTION

Today is a day to spend time with the Lord in any way you desire. You may choose to meditate on a Scripture from the previous week, summarize your thoughts, list your questions, or just sit quietly with the Lord. You may wish to read your Bible.

Use the space provided below to journal, sketch, or otherwise record your thoughts.

Handwrite a Scripture or phrase. Or just take this time to sit quietly with God.

Week 6

A sacrifice to be real must cost, must hurt, and must empty
ourselves. Give yourself fully to God. He will use you to accomplish
great things on the condition that you believe much more in his
love than in your weakness.
—Mother Teresa

This week your focus will be on the nature of sacrifice and
what God is calling you to offer Him.

Day 1
FAITHFULNESS

When her husband Elkanah went up with all his family to offer the
annual sacrifice to the Lord and to fulfill his vow, Hannah did not
go. She said to her husband, "After the boy is weaned, I will take
him and present him before the Lord, and he will live there always."
—1 Samuel 1:21–22

This week we will focus on 1 Samuel 1:21–2:11. To set the stage
for the next days of our study, read these verses from your Bible. The
area below is reserved for you to record notes, questions, and ideas as
you read.

_____

_____

_____

_____

_____

_____

_____

_____

_____

We have spent the last weeks with Hannah. We saw a broken, barren woman rise up with joy as she learned to trust and surrender. Did you write the word *faithful* in your notes? Faithfulness is the ongoing theme in the relationship between Hannah and God. Not only was God faithful to Hannah, but Hannah was faithful to God.

God blessed Hannah with the son she yearned to bear. He chose to answer her by allowing her to conceive and give birth to this beautiful baby boy named Samuel. But then it was Hannah's turn to practice the faithfulness of her God. Back in 1 Samuel 1:11, Hannah vowed that if God gave her a son, she would dedicate him to the Lord's service for all his days.

Now when I read that verse the first several times, I assumed she raised him to go into ministry later in life, to love the Lord and serve him in adulthood. I assumed that Hannah spent her days caring for Samuel and teaching him the ways of God. But that was not the case. Actually, it was at approximately age three that Hannah took Samuel to the temple and dedicated him to the Lord.

My children were also dedicated as infants. That simply meant that as a family, we vowed to raise them in the knowledge and love of God. Each time we gave birth to a child, my husband and I bought sweet little outfits and took our precious babies before the church, where we made a public vow to take them to church and do our best to model service to God throughout their upbringing. In return the church promised to support our children as they grew.

But Hannah's dedication of Samuel was significantly different from the traditional dedication today. How did it differ as stated in 1 Samuel 1:22–2:11?

_____

_____

_____

_____

That's right. Hannah took her son to the temple and left him there to be raised by Eli, the chief priest. From that time forward, Samuel assisted Eli, who instructed him in the Scriptures, practices, and responsibilities of the tabernacle. Samuel *literally* grew up *in* the church.

Yes, God is faithful to us, and He wants us, as His children, to take on the attributes of His character. Hannah made a promise to God, and in this instance, He asked her to make good on her promise. Why? Because God had a plan for both Hannah and Samuel.

Hannah learned to totally trust God as she handed her son over to Eli; thus she displayed faithfulness to God. And Samuel was raised to be one of the greatest prophets of the Lord. With all my heart I believe Hannah would have faithfully served God, even if He had chosen not to bless her with a son, because she had come to know God personally.

Make It Personal

Have you, like Hannah, ever made a vow to God? Have you been faithful to fulfill your vow?

_____

_____

God's faithfulness is not always evidenced in prayers answered the way we desire. Can you think of a time in your life that God answered your prayer in a way you didn't expect, and yet revealed His faithfulness?

_____

_____

_____

_____

I am in no way suggesting you or I are in any position to expect God to answer our prayers the way we would like because we promise to be faithful to Him, nor am I saying we should ever try to strike a bargain with God. Yet Hannah's openness and answered prayer revealed God's faithfulness. The appropriate response to His faithfulness is our faithfulness to Him in the form of obedience and gratitude.

And So, We Pray

Dear Lord, You are faithful beyond measure. Your decisions are made with infinite wisdom and divine purpose. Lord, like Hannah, I want to be faithful to You. Help me to do the hard things when You call upon me. Enable me by the power of Your Spirit to respond to Your faithfulness with gratitude and faithfulness to Your call. Amen.

Day 1 Discussion Question

Discuss where you have seen the faithfulness of God displayed in your life or the life of another. God's faithfulness to Hannah changed her significantly. Has His faithfulness to you moved you to acts of service and faithfulness? If so, how?

Day 2
SACRIFICE

"I prayed for this child, and the LORD has granted me what I asked of him. So now I give him to the LORD. For his whole life he will be given over to the LORD." And he worshiped the LORD there.
—1 Samuel 1:27–28

Read 1 Samuel 1:24-28. Describe *sacrifice* as you see it evidenced in these verses.

_____

_____

_____

_____

_____

_____

Merriam-Webster Dictionary defines sacrifice as "the act of offering to a deity something precious." I'm not sure I can even begin to understand the sacrifice Hannah made. I can't comprehend how she felt the day she went to the temple to offer her son in service to the Lord.

Though Scripture doesn't expound on the details of her handing Samuel over to the priest, I feel safe in assuming this was no small sacrifice. I'm sure her heart was torn, her eyes were wet, and once again her arms ached to hold her precious little boy. No scrapbook to flip through. No Instagram posts to peruse. No Facetime. She offered her son and left with only what she held in her heart. Yet Hannah peacefully gave this one and only son to God in dedication to His service.

Hannah did not offer her son out of obligation to fulfill a vow she had made in haste. I believe Hannah knew full well when she cried out at the temple steps that she would follow through on her end of this promise.

I believe that because Hannah's heart was shattered, she turned to the one and only One who could put her life back together again. Hannah had not only determined to dedicate her son to the Lord, but she was determined to offer her life to Him as well. In the wait, Hannah had learned that God's love would sustain her even when her empty arms and her broken heart ached.

Hannah's sacrifice was given with a true heart. She knew God, His faithfulness, and the healing that only He could give. Her sacrifice hurt deeply and cost her everything.

My friend, this is the kind of sacrifice God desires. God wants a sacrifice that costs us, a sacrifice that is meaningful and from a heart of gratitude.

Make It Personal

I have to admit that in light of Hannah's sacrifice, my own sacrifices seem trivial at best. But God is not in the comparison business. Remember how we talked about His unique love for us. This is also true of our entire relationship with God. My story is my story. No one else can tell it like I do, would live it out like I am, or will understand it the way I do.

My greatest sacrifice to the Lord has been control. I loved being in control of my life. My theory was to follow the rules and make good decisions. Keep everyone happy and help others make good decisions. Fix others' problems and heal their hurts . . . that is, until my world fell apart—so much so that I can honestly say I was stressed to the max and found myself in the behavioral unit of the hospital for a week.

At that time I had to sacrifice everything and everyone I loved for the simple grace of a God who could handle what I was never meant to handle alone. I offered the Lord control of my life and the lives of the ones I loved. It may sound easy for some, but I believe it to be the hardest thing I've ever done.

What true sacrifice have you offered to the Lord in response to His faithfulness? Do you tithe what is left over, or do you give until it hurts? Do you give to others freely? Will you offer Him your bitterness or your unforgiveness? Is He asking you to relinquish your spouse, not literally, but spiritually?

What call has God put on your heart? Pray about your understanding of sacrifice and record any thoughts here.

_____

_____

_____

_____

And So, We Pray

Dear Jesus, You fully understand the meaning of sacrifice. You gave all so I could have eternal life. You spared no expense to purchase my life as You left Your throne in heaven to suffer and die as the sacrifice that covered my sin.

Heavenly Father, make me aware of the areas in my life where I am going my way instead of living as a sacrifice, holy and pleasing to You. Amen.

Day 2 Discussion Question

Hannah's sacrifice to the Lord was one of great magnitude. It is not one we are all called to make by offering our toddlers to full-time service in the tabernacle. But what are some of the daily sacrifices you are called to offer?

Day 3
REJOICE IN THE LORD

Rejoice in the Lord always. I will say it again: Rejoice.
—Philippians 4:4

Today we will look at Hannah's prayer. Begin by reading the prayer in its entirety in 1 Samuel 2:1–11 from your Bible. Use the area below to record notes, questions, or thoughts you have as you read.

_____

_____

_____

_____

_____

_____

_____

We must make the connection between 1 Samuel 1:28 and Hannah's subsequent prayer. If you are using the NIV translation, verse 28 says, "And he worshiped the LORD there." However the New King James Version says, "And *they* worshiped the LORD there."

This implies that Hannah (and her family) worshiped the Lord at the tabernacle where she was leaving her son in Eli's care. Hannah offered this prayer on the very day she left her son, knowing he would never again live in her home.

Now read 1 Samuel 2:1 again. How does Hannah's prayer begin?

Hannah rejoiced. Scripture says she rejoiced in the Lord. Hannah didn't rejoice in the fact that she was leaving her son. Who would? Hannah rejoiced in the Lord. Hannah's ability to worship God on possibly the hardest day of her life teaches us that even in the darkest, most desperate situations, we can rejoice *in* God.

Like Hannah, I have been in some dark, desperate places in my life. Hannah's commitment to the Lord is humbling to me. I can honestly say my response to trials wasn't always one of rejoicing in the Lord. I was often looking to find a way out of the situation, begging God to change things and rescue me or my loved ones. Unlike Hannah, my eyes were laser focused on the ugliness of my circumstances, not on the Lord.

But thankfully, through my friendship with Hannah, she has taught my heart to lean on God and let Him be my joy and peace in the middle of pain and chaos.

> "Then Hannah prayed and said: 'My heart rejoices in the Lord; in the Lord my horn is lifted high. My mouth boasts over my enemies, for I delight in your deliverance'" (1 Samuel 2:1).

Hannah definitely responded to God with praise. She was thankful. Her heart and eyes were opened to the sovereignty and majesty of God. She said that her heart rejoiced and her "horn" was lifted high.

The picture of her horn being lifted high is the image of strength. Just like the horn of an ox or a steer represents its strength, Hannah boasted in the strength of God. How else could she permanently give her child to another without the supernatural strength of God Almighty? She had walked this journey with the Lord and had seen His strength as He drew her from a pit of pain and barrenness. She had seen His sovereignty and His justice. Hannah praised the Lord because He is good.

As I read this one small verse, I stand in awe of Hannah. She had come so far—from broken to bold and beautiful.

As our study began we found Hannah in tears, sprawled out on the tabernacle steps crying out in desperation and pain. But today we find a woman of praise and rejoicing. Can you see her? I can. I see her standing at the altar of the tabernacle, arms raised, eyes closed, with praise on her lips and peace in her heart. I can hear the silent song of her heart echo throughout the sanctuary as those in attendance look to her with a desire to know the Lord and praise Him in such a way. No longer was she mistaken as a woman influenced by drink, but rather a woman reflecting the grace of God.

First Samuel 2:2 reads, "There is no one holy like the Lord; there is no one besides you; there is no Rock like our God."

Why could Hannah rejoice in the Lord on this most difficult of days?

Hannah rejoiced because she had come to know that God is holy and faithful despite her circumstances. She knew God was on her side and nothing could overcome her. Hannah's strength was in the Lord.

Make It Personal

After intimately encountering God through depression and devastation, the next trial came, the next battle against cancer in both my son and husband. I stood taller, stronger this time, knowing God would see us through. Maybe He'd answer the way I wanted or maybe He would not, but either way, I knew God would not take his eyes off us for even one second.

This time I wasn't broken. This time I stood tall on His shoulders. This time I offered up control in exchange for all of God.

When have you, like Hannah, had to face a difficult trial? What was your response in the trial? What was your response after the trial had passed?

_____

_____

_____

_____

What do you need to do to prepare yourself to rejoice in the Lord through your current trial or in the next storm?

_____

_____

_____

_____

As you seek to understand what it truly means to be joyful in the Lord, spend today meditating on these verses:

Give thanks in all circumstances; for this is God's will for you in Christ Jesus. (1 Thessalonians 5:18)

May my meditation be pleasing to him, as I rejoice in the LORD. (Psalm 104:34)

And a beautiful verse that calls our hearts to praise even in the bleakest of circumstances:

"Though the fig tree does not bud and there are no grapes on the vines, though the olive crop fails and the fields produce no food, though there are no sheep in the pen and no cattle in the stalls, yet I will rejoice in the LORD, I will be joyful in God my Savior" (Habakkuk 3:17–18).

And So, We Pray
Dear heavenly Father, forgive me for the times when I have taken my eyes off You and allowed my situation to overtake me. Though my situation may be difficult, I want to know You and to be so fixed on You that my heart can sing praises even in the storms of life. Amen.

Write your prayer here today.

Day 3 Discussion Question

Discuss the idea of rejoicing in all situations. How might you help one another be joyful in your trials?

Day 4
JUSTICE AND VICTORY

Do not keep talking so proudly or let your mouth speak such
arrogance, for the LORD is a God who knows,
and by him deeds are weighed.
—1 Samuel 2:3

It wasn't all that long ago that we were studying Peninnah's
vindictive spirit. We read how she constantly tormented Hannah,
provoking her even to tears. Peninnah sought to bring Hannah low and
intended to harm her. And for a time, she succeeded. Now as we read
Hannah's prayer, we see that the tides have turned. Hannah stands in
victory, yet not as we may understand victory to be.

Read Hannah's prayer found in 1 Samuel 2:1–10.

Then Hannah prayed and said:
    My heart rejoices in the LORD; in the LORD my horn is lifted high.
My mouth boasts over my enemies, for I delight in your deliverance.
    There is no one holy like the LORD; there is no one besides you;
there is no Rock like our God.

Do not keep talking so proudly or let your mouth speak such arrogance, for the LORD is a God who knows, and by him deeds are weighed.

The bows of the warriors are broken, but those who stumbled are armed with strength. Those who were full hire themselves out for food, but those who were hungry are hungry no more. She who was barren has borne seven children, but she who has had many sons pines away.

The LORD brings death and makes alive; he brings down to the grave and raises up. The LORD sends poverty and wealth; he humbles and he exalts. He raises the poor from the dust and lifts the needy from the ash heap; he seats them with princes and has them inherit a throne of honor.

For the foundations of the earth are the LORD's; on them he has set the world. He will guard the feet of his faithful servants, but the wicked will be silenced in the place of darkness.

It is not by strength that one prevails; those who oppose the LORD will be broken. The Most High will thunder from heaven; the LORD will judge the ends of the earth.

He will give strength to his king and exalt the horn of his anointed.

As you read Hannah's words, what is your first impression? What thoughts do you have about these words? If you struggled to understand portions of the passage, you may want to read them in another version or search commentaries online.

_____

_____

_____

_____

Hannah had every reason to retaliate. She had every reason to say or do unkind things to Peninnah in response to the evil that was shown her.

You've been there, right? Someone hurts you, so you want to lash out and make sure he or she feels the pain you feel. You just want to take matters into your hands and make sure justice is served. Yet Hannah teaches us a better way. Her victory is not getting back at Peninnah and having the last laugh. Rather she shows us the way to Christ's peace, which is in knowing that God is just. He will not let sin go unpunished. He will make sure there is justice.

Hannah wasn't boasting over Peninnah in a prideful way. She was boasting in the fact that God would handle all matters as He saw fit. Hannah was free to live without contempt, bitterness, and strife. Hannah was bragging about the sovereignty and justness of God.

Hannah's wisdom is beautiful. She knew God would judge Peninnah, but she also knew God would judge her, so she left the justice to Him and kept her hands clean. She didn't retaliate. She didn't put Peninnah in her place. She didn't even use a tiny drop of sarcasm to prove her point.

Hannah was a woman of grace and beauty. She was a woman who not only believed God had strength and power, she also believed He would use it. Thus she didn't have to use her force to right a wrong. Hannah stood in victory because she allowed God to fight for her.

Make It Personal

My friendship with Hannah has spared me the foolishness of getting even. Often when I've had the chance to have my last say, drive the knife in a little deeper, or say that one small sarcastic line, I've remembered Hannah's grace—grace she personally received from God, author of grace.

God's lavish grace to Hannah not only changed the way Hannah reacted to her enemy, it also changed the way I respond to those who are intent on hurting me.

Grace is contagious.

What are you personally hearing God say about retaliation and justice?

_____

_____

_____

Are there instances that come to mind that you now believe you mishandled? Are you being led to make amends?

_____

_____

_____

Because of Hannah's lesson, what will you do differently the next time you are unjustly treated?

_____

_____

_____

And So, We Pray

Today pen your own prayer to God. What has He said to you about justice and victory? What issues or injustices is He asking you to let go of so you can live in freedom, knowing He will justly handle the matter? If you have mishandled a situation, ask God to forgive you and seek to handle future issues with His help.

_____

_____

_____

_____

_____

_____

_____

_____

Day 4 Discussion Question

Women can be cold and cutting, especially when someone wrongs us personally or wounds a family member. Mama Bear is sometimes hard to contain. Yet God calls us to a different kind of justice. What would that look like in action?

Day 5

In Service
to the Lord

Serve the Lord with gladness:
come before his presence with singing.
—Psalm 100:2 NKJV

Our time together is drawing to a close, but not without one final word from Hannah's story. Today is the culmination of six weeks of lessons from Hannah, six weeks of self-reflection and hopefully discussion and prayer with your accountability partner or small group. Today Hannah's lesson will show us how to implement all she has taught us.

Hannah was barren and broken. Her heart ached for a child. She longed to swaddle a precious son and feel the warmth of his little body and his breath upon her skin. Hannah longed to be a mother.

Hannah was mistreated, berated, and beaten down by the one woman in her life who could have shown compassion and care for her. Jealousy and rivalry sent Hannah to her knees in agony of mind and spirit.

Yet because Hannah sought the Lord, she was not destroyed. She was strengthened and redeemed from broken to beautiful. Her messes are used to this very day to proclaim the glory of her God and her Savior, Jesus Christ.

Hannah knew the source of her strength. She felt His resurrection power within her very soul, and out of gratitude she responded with praise, obedience, and service to the Lord.

Take a moment and reread Hannah's story from beginning to end (1 Samuel 1:1–2:11). Let the story replay in its entirety. Watch as redemption unfolds. Envision Hannah rising from her place of devastation on the tabernacle floor to become a woman who boldly stands, arms outstretched in praise, in the very tabernacle where her story began. It is there she not only offered her life but also her son in service to the Lord.

Don't skip that request. Take a moment to drink in the beauty of Hannah's story one more time. Why? Because she will give you the courage to complete your next task. Her story, by God's design, will empower you to rise from your ashes, leave your messes in His hands, and live in service to the King of Kings.

"Then Elkanah returned home to Ramah without Samuel. And the boy served the LORD by assisting Eli the priest" (1 Samuel 2:11 NLT).

Our final message from Hannah's story is one of service. Elkanah returned home with his beautiful wife Hannah in the service of the Lord. How do I know this? I know because this kind of sacrifice is not offered without a heart that seeks to honor God. And I believe that offering didn't stop at the tabernacle altar.

The offering of their son was a testimony to their love and dedication to serving God faithfully. Even on the most difficult of days, Hannah and her family lived in service to the Lord.

Now it's your turn.

Make It Personal

What is God calling you to sacrifice for His service? What is He asking of you? Is it a greater tithe, a job change, the sacrifice of time to build your relationship with Him, or devotion of time to serve in a place of ministry?

If you are unsure of the call He has placed on your life, don't be alarmed. Just continue to walk with Him as Hannah has taught you, and He will faithfully lead you from your turmoil into His glory.

_____

_____

_____

_____

_____

_____

And So, We Pray

Dear Jesus,

_____

_____

_____

_____

_____

Amen and amen.

Day 5 Discussion Question

Hannah lived a life of service to the Lord. What do you feel called to do in response to God's work in your life?

Day 6

FAREWELL

Here's another way to put it: You're here to be light, bringing out
the God-colors in the world. God is not a secret to be kept. We're
going public with this, as public as a city on a hill. If I make you
light-bearers, you don't think I'm going to hide you under a bucket,
do you? I'm putting you on a light stand. Now that I've put you
there on a hilltop, on a light stand—shine! Keep open house; be
generous with your lives. By opening up to others, you'll prompt
people to open up with God, this generous Father in heaven.
—Matthew 5:14–16 MSG

Today we end this time with one another. I must say that I am
so proud of you for continuing to the end of this study, and I'm confident
that you have been changed by the power of the Holy Spirit. Though
today is the last day we will spend together in this book, I believe it will
not be the last day we will spend together.

God has written the story of Hannah in our hearts as we have studied
together over the last six weeks. We have come to know each other in a

deeper, more personal way, and friendships like this don't just end. We will be together in glory.

I pray that you will remember Hannah and the precious lessons from her life's story. I pray that you will continue to grow in your relationship with the Lord and with others—and that, like Hannah, you will share your story of how God is taking you from broken to bold and beautiful.

Until we meet again, my friend.

Mary

Make It Personal

What are you going to take away from this study of God's Word? What lessons will you apply to your life?

_____

_____

_____

_____

_____

_____

And So, We Pray

Dear Jesus,

_____

_____

_____

Amen and amen.

Day 6 Discussion Questions

What are you going to take away from this study of God's Word? What lessons will you apply to your life?

Day 7
Rest and Reflection

Today is a day to spend time with the Lord in any way you desire. You may choose to meditate on a Scripture from the previous week, summarize your thoughts, list your questions, or just sit quietly with the Lord. You may wish to read your Bible.

Use the space below to journal, sketch, or otherwise record your thoughts. Handwrite a Scripture or phrase. Or just take this time to sit quietly with God.

GOD FIRST FRIENDS
COVENANT

I am a God First Friend. I will seek to put God first in my life by continually studying His Word and applying it to my life. I will walk in relationship with Jesus as my Savior and my Friend.

> Love the LORD your God with all your heart and with all your soul and with all your strength. These commandments that I give you today are to be on your hearts. Impress them on your children. **Talk about them when you sit at home and when you walk along the road, when you lie down and when you get up.** Tie them as symbols on your hands and bind them on your foreheads. Write them on the doorframes of your houses and on your gates. (Deuteronomy 6:5–9)

As a God First Friend, I will live for God alone and base my life on His truth. I will prayerfully speak the truth even when it is difficult, ugly, or unpopular. When I lie down at the end of the day, I will sleep with God's peace in my heart because I have walked in right relationship with my Lord. My actions will reflect my decision to live as a follower of Christ.

On the contrary, we speak as those approved by God to be entrusted with the Gospel. We are not trying to please people but God, who tests our hearts. (1 Thessalonians 2:4)

Finally, brothers and sisters, whatever is true, whatever is noble, whatever is right, whatever is pure, whatever is lovely, whatever is admirable—if anything is excellent or praiseworthy—think about such things. (Philippians 4:8)

Do your best to present yourself to God as one approved, a worker who does not need to be ashamed and who correctly handles the word of truth. (2 Timothy 2:15)

So then, each of us will give an account of ourselves to God. (Romans 14:12)

As a God First Friend, I will truthfully, confidently, and boldly share my story as a testimony of God's faithfulness.

I thank God through Jesus for every one of you. That's first. People everywhere keep telling me about your lives of faith, and every time I hear them, I thank him. And God, whom I so love to worship and serve by spreading the good news of his Son—the Message!—knows that every time I think of you in my prayers, which is practically all the time, I ask him to clear the way for me to come and see you. The longer this waiting goes on, the deeper the ache. I so want to be there to deliver God's gift in person and watch you grow stronger right before my eyes! But don't think I'm not expecting to get something out of this, too! You have as much to give me as I do to you. (Romans 1:11–12 MSG)

As a God First Friend, I will live humbly, always remembering that I am a life redeemed, a sinner forgiven only by the grace of God, and a mess made whole. I will not forget my past, because it has made me who I am today. However, I will joyfully remember it so that I will have a humble heart and not think of myself more highly than I should. Remembering my past will help me see others through the eyes of understanding and compassion.

He has shown you, O mortal, what is good. And what does the Lord require of you? To act justly and to love mercy and to walk humbly with your God. (Micah 6:8)

As a God First Friend, I will hold my GFFs accountable to God's truth. I will encourage them to be the best princesses, wives, mothers, daughters, and friends that they can be. I will rebuke them in love and prayerfully receive their correction. I will praise with them in joy and love them with an everlasting love because I am their GFF.

A friend loves at all times, and a brother is born for a time of adversity. (Proverbs 17:17)

Whoever rebukes a person will in the end gain favor rather than one who has a flattering tongue. (Proverbs 28:23)

A person shouldn't stop being kind to a friend. Anyone who does that stops showing respect for the Mighty One. (Job 6:14 NIRV)

Finally, brothers and sisters, rejoice! Strive for full restoration, encourage one another, be of one mind, live in peace. And the God of love and peace will be with you. (2 Corinthians 13:11)

Dear Lord, I commit my life to You. I will, with the leading of the Holy Spirit, walk this life with You as my Lord, Savior, and Friend. I want to live putting God First in all I do. Please bless the relationships we have as GFFs. Through Your Spirit we will hold each other up and be obedient to do Your work.

Signature _____

Date _____

ORDER INFORMATION

REDEMPTION
PRESS

To order additional copies of this book, please visit
www.redemption-press.com.
Also available on Amazon.com and BarnesandNoble.com
or by calling toll-free 1-844-2REDEEM.

- Hannah -
- She let the world determine her worth
- God will use our difficulties to display His glory!
- What is a mess - bad decisions - insecurities, someone else's bad decisions, someone else hurting us - or someone else hurt indirect, for us!
- Romans 8:28 - God is working for us!